The Cantatas of
Luigi Rossi
Analysis and Thematic Index

Studies in Musicology

George Buelow, Series Editor
Professor of Musicology
Indiana University

Other Titles in This Series

The Cantatas of Luigi Rossi

Analysis and Thematic Index

Vol. 1

by
Eleanor Caluori

RESEARCH PRESS

Produced and distributed by
UMI Research Press
an imprint of
University Microfilms International
Ann Arbor, Michigan 48106

A revision of the author's thesis,
Brandeis University, 1971

Library of Congress Cataloging in Publication Data

Caluori, Eleanor.
The cantatas of Luigi Rossi.

(Studies in musicology ; no. 41)
Revision of thesis (Ph.D.)—Brandeis University, 1971.
Bibliography: p.
Includes index.
1. Rossi, Luigi, 1598-1653. Cantatas.   I. Title.
II. Series.

ML410.R76C3 1981   782.8'2'0924   81-4749
ISBN 0-8357-1171-4 (set)   AACR2
ISBN 0-8357-1191-9 (v.1)

54,506

Contents

Acknowledgments

I am grateful to many people for their generous help while I gathered material for this book and during its writing. In the initial stages of my work, I received good advice from Federico Ghisi and David Burrows. Villa Schifanoia in Florence and my cousin Antonio Miscione in Rome offered me their hospitality while I worked in libraries in those cities. Geneviève Thibault welcomed me into her home while I examined her entire collection of manuscripts. The librarians Albert Vander Linden (Brussels Conservatory), François Lesure (Bibliothèque Nationale, Paris), H. R. Wing (Christ Church, Oxford), and many others clarified puzzling questions and responded promptly to my numerous communications.

Owen Jander's enthusiasm was uplifting. He, Gloria Rose, Edwin Hanley, David Wood, Arthur Hills, and Colin Timms were exceedingly cooperative in sharing their knowledge of the manuscript sources. Richard Macnutt also made known to me a manuscript once owned by the music historian M. Pincherle.

Paul Brainard generously spent many hours reading and annotating the several drafts of this book. To him I am indebted for innumerable valuable recommendations and suggestions that have considerably benefited both the form and content of this work. Claudette Charbonneau and Ethel Thurston also read the text and gave me helpful criticism.

For their loving encouragement and interest I thank my parents, my husband and my friends, especially Louise Talma.

Introduction

Luigi Rossi was born in Torremaggiore in Puglia circa 1598. There is little biographical information on Rossi's early years. We know that he lived at the Neapolitan court for 14 years, having possibly entered a court chapel at the age of eight or nine. During these years in Naples he was a pupil of Jean de Macque.

Luigi entered the service of Marc'Antonio Borghese in Rome in 1621. Also in the employ of this family was Costanza de Ponte, a celebrated harpist, who became Luigi's wife on 3 July 1627. In 1633 Luigi succeeded Arcangelo Lori as organist at the church of San Luigi dei Francesi, a position once held by his master Jean de Macque, and one that he retained until his death. A brief visit of six months to the court of Ferdinand II dei Medici in Florence in 1635 marked his first appearance in the aristocratic courts north of Rome.

By 1640 Luigi had earned a place among the best musicians of his time. He was named the head of the Roman school of musicians by Severo Bonini in his famous *Discorso*, and received other significant accolades. In 1641 he became a "musico" of Cardinal Antonio Barberini, ardent and influential patron of the arts. The Cardinal appointed Luigi in 1642 to compose the chief work to be produced in his Teatro delle Quattro Fontane during the carnival season. The performance of *Il Palazzo Incantato* attracted much attention. The following year Rossi joined his patron, then serving as a papal ambassador to Romagna in Bologna, and remained there for an entire year. In 1644 Luigi held an Academy in his home in Rome in which the best virtuosi in the city participated. Many musicians were influenced by Luigi Rossi, among them Atto Melani, Marc'Antonio Pasqualini, Loreto Vittori, Filippo Vitali, Lorenzo Sances, Antonio Francesco Tenaglia, Carlo Caproli, Mario Savioni, Leonora Baroni and Thomas Gobert. The enthusiasm that Luigi's cantatas inspired in his colleagues possibly accounts for their wide diffusion. The cantatas of no contemporary are found in as many concordances as are those of Luigi.

With the departure of the Barberini for France in 1645, Luigi's opportunities to compose another opera for the Teatre delle Quattro Fontane ended. But another opportunity came from the court of France. Invited directly by Cardinal Mazarin, Luigi arrived in Paris in June 1646. During his year at the French court, Luigi composed his second opera, *Orfeo*, served Anne of Austria by composing cantatas for the private concerts in her salon, and collaborated with French musicians in the entertainments presented at Fontainebleau during the summer months.

The preparations for the performance of *Orfeo* were extensive and costly. The six-hour performance on 2 March 1647 was a sensational event written of in numerous contemporary letters and journals. The extravagance of its production caused much criticism of the court among the populace who were living for the most part in miserable conditions.

No theatrical spectacles were produced by Italian artists during Luigi's second sojourn in Paris (January 1648–September 1649). It is not known what Luigi's activities in France were during this visit. Since the situation in Paris was not favorable for Italian musicians, Rossi joined Cardinal Antonio at a castle near Lyon at the beginning of October 1649. The date of his return to Rome is unknown; it may have been the beginning of the Holy Year 1650. Luigi Rossi died in his home the morning of 20 February 1653. Most of his possessions were bequeathed to his youngest brother Giovan Carlo, who was also a composer and organist. Costanza, Luigi's wife, had died in November 1646 while Luigi was in Paris composing *Orfeo*.[1]

It was the winter of 1961 in Florence when I received David Burrows's letter recommending Luigi Rossi to me. I was already enthusiastic about the seventeenth-century cantata.[2] Prompted by Professor Federico Ghisi, I had transcribed and studied the contents of MS Magliabecchi XIX 26. But it was the anonymous setting of the text of Carissimi's cantata, *O voi ch'in arid ossa*, that first absorbed my attention. With the anonymous version copied measure for measure below Carissimi's setting, Professor Ghisi and I were able to make an interesting comparative analysis. We concluded that the anonymous version was not another and earlier setting by Carissimi, but the work of a probably older contemporary. I wondered if it were not possibly the music of a composer represented in the MS with another cantata. My attention became centered on the anonymous piece *Da perfida speranza*, and I determined to find its composer. At this point I became aware of the urgent need for a comprehensive index of the entire repertory. I was intent upon organizing the vast amount of music chaotically scattered in numerous libraries into an order that would permit easy collation, comparison of the sources, and possible identification of the composers. I proceeded to index all the cantata MSS in Florence containing the repertory of the mid-century. Meanwhile I had found a source in Venice that attributed the cantata *Da perfida speranza* to Carissimi and had also learned from Ghislanzoni's catalogue of Luigi's cantatas of the attribution of the same piece in other sources to Luigi Rossi. What a fine composer Luigi Rossi must have been that his music was associated with Carissimi's, I thought; and I firmly decided to collect and study his cantatas.

When David Burrows learned of my decision, he wrote back: "It was with some feelings of guilt that I learned of your decision for Rossi, because I have a fair notion of the labor it's going to involve. . . . But when you have finished, I'm sure your results ought to be important because Rossi is very close to the heart of the cantata matter."

My first work, the thematic catalogue, was several years in the making because of the great number of manuscripts I examined and collated.[3] I found that I could not rely on printed catalogues, when they were available, so I visited most of the libraries holding cantata manuscripts. I determined to know each cantata and to study each from various points of view, and therefore I copied out many of them. In some instances I also noted all of the variants in the several sources. In every case I copied the cantata text to find its poetic form. When I discovered settings by other composers, I often copied these. As I worked I became convinced of Luigi's[4] genius and I saw that David Burrows was right—my work took me "very close to the heart of the cantata matter."

The cantatas have been inadequately researched. Whereas the biographical chapters in Ghislanzoni's monograph[5] are excellent, the stylistic analysis is deficient. The discussion is predominantly aesthetic. The structural aspects of the music are not treated in much detail. There is no published discussion where one can learn the facts about the compositional devices and stylistic elements in Luigi's cantatas. Furthermore, there are inaccuracies in the published analyses which give a distorted view of the subject. For example, Bukofzer states that strophic variation was the major means of creating unity in the works of Luigi Rossi.[6] This could not possibly be the case because strophic variation occurs infrequently, and is never a primary means of achieving unity.

In none of the available literature could I find adequate answers to several questions: How are the forms of cantatas identifiable? How are they articulated? What are the characteristic features in terms of repetition, tonal organization, cadences, proportionate lengths, use of refrains and ritornelli, place of sequences, modulations, melismatic passages, juxtaposition of melodic styles, kinds and use of recitative, recurring mottoes and migratory melodies? What are the features in terms of text design?

Therefore, I decided that my study should focus on problems of formal construction in Luigi's cantatas. The 294 cantatas that I studied are those I am convinced are Luigi's on stylistic as well as bibliographical grounds.[7] I found that the cantatas separate into six groups: the binary, the rounded binary, the ternary, the rondo, the lament, and the aria di più parti, a free form of several parts.[8] The first four of these groups, which account for the larger number of the cantatas—216—have clear, well-defined formal designs. The fifth group, 17 cantatas, consists of the laments, a category hitherto undefined.[9] These are longer than the cantatas of the first four groups, are mostly in recitative, and are usually composed of three main divisions determined in part by the textual structure. Whereas the shorter cantatas are characterized by a bel canto style of melody and by immediately apparent designs, the laments recall the earlier austere and dramatic monodies. But Luigi imparts a new sense of organization to the old laments.

The last of the six groups, 61 cantatas, consists of arie di più parti. Unlike some cantatas among the other groups, the arie di più parti bear no relation to the late monodies in their formal structure, but look forward. Here we find the parent of the cantata of the sixties and seventies. In the arie di più parti the underlying principles of construction are far from obvious. In each, the succession of musical events is unique. The one basic characteristic of this group is diversity. Each aria di più parti presents a unique combination of ariette, recitatives, recitative-aria pairs and strophes of octosyllables or hexasyllables "in aria," a combination of all, or of any three or two. There is no a priori formal design.

The arie di più parti cannot be properly called composite forms.[10] There are only two cantatas, *S'era alquanto*[11] and *Compatite*, that are made of several complete and independent sections. None of the other arie di più parti is a truly composite form because none of the distinct sections is independent. According to the use of the word in the seventeenth-century edition of Lotti's poetry, many of the arie di più parti could be called "canzonette." Here "canzonette" are poems for music of several strophes differing in kind and structure, implying a succession of recitatives and arias, a variety of forms with or without refrain.[12]

Rather than "canzonette" I prefer to use the term "arie di più parti," which I found on the title page of the MS *I* BC, V/289, referring to cantatas of diverse and multiple sections. While "arie di più parti" names the basic feature of all the cantatas of the group, "canzonetta" fits only those pieces whose texts are extensions of the short cantatas in subject and structure and which are not related to the laments. Many of the arie di più parti are not canzonette because their texts are modeled after the lament.

Also among the arie di più parti are several cantatas that I call the "series" cantatas.[13] These are not strophic ariettas, nor are they composites of several contrasting independent parts differently constructed.

Nor are they a succession of aria and recitative movements. The "series" cantatas are composed of a chain of similar short one-unit strophes, each of approximately the same length and each referring in some way to the musical material of the others. They are related by the quotation of one or two phrases, usually with new words; by their tonal organization—often the modulations occur in the same or nearly the same order; by metric similarity, and by recurring cadences.

The six classifications I have used are not the same as those found in other discussions of the cantata forms. Ghislanzoni recognizes that the three categories of structural types given by Bukofzer—the aria cantata, the refrain cantata and the rondo cantata—do not adequately represent the forms of the cantatas, but he offers no other precise classifications.[14] In his catalogue, he uses the terms "canzone strofica" or "canzone con refrain," as the case may be, for most of the cantatas of my first four groups. But others among these same cantatas are called "canzone-cantata," "canzone-aria," occasionally "canzonetta," and "aria," a designation that is also given to some of the arie di più parti. In general he calls the arie di più parti and the laments "cantata," but he does not limit the term to these groups, for even a few binary pieces are named "cantata."

It is obvious that these classifications, which are not consistently applied, are far from satisfactory. Though Bukofzer's suggested three groups seem more clearly delineated, they fail to account for much of the internal variety of the genre. If aria cantata, which "consists of only one aria repeated for every stanza of the text," includes all the short cantatas that are not rondos, it includes binary, binary with closing refrain, rounded binary and ternary cantatas. The second category, the refrain cantata, is that in which "only the middle part changes while the first section serves as refrain." But the example Bukofzer cites, *Difenditi, Amore*, is a rounded binary cantata. While the definition seems to denote a rondo form, the term "refrain cantata" itself seems to define a cantata within which a lyric phrase recurs periodically—a category which would include three different kinds of form: the laments, the arie di più parti whose structure is similar to the lament with recurring refrain, and the arie di più parti having a unit articulated by an arioso refrain. But these types, according to Bukofzer, would fall under the third category, the "rondo cantata," "the most complex type . . . in which the various recitative and arioso sections are held together by a short aria repeated at intervals in rondo fashion." Thus the category comprises several diverse forms, but it does not include the simple rondo (this is a "refrain cantata").

"Strophic variation" has also been used to describe the formal structure of the cantata, but in Luigi's cantatas it is nothing more than a compositional procedure infrequently employed to embellish one or another of the short closed forms.[15] Strophic variation is the repetition of a unit or an entire arietta with new text and with some melodic and rhythmic alterations. The bass line remains essentially the same, usually undergoing only slight rhythmic changes and some additions of passing and neighboring tones. Whether a binary arietta or a rondo is strophic or strophically varied does not determine its design.

After having seen and copied a much larger repertory of cantatas than was accessible to either Ghislanzoni or Bukofzer, I find that the classifications that I have chosen—binary, rondo, ternary, rounded binary, lament and aria di più parti—clearly represent the structural designs of the cantatas.

The forms used by Luigi are not apportioned as they are in the works of his contemporaries. Only one fifth of Luigi's cantatas are arie di più parti, as against nearly half of Carissimi's and Caproli's. But these composers lived after Luigi and were active in the sixties when the aria di più parti was the preferred form. It is true that the rondo form in the cantatas of Luigi and Carissimi is found in nearly the same proportion— about one fourth—but this form comprises only one eighth of Caproli's cantatas. On the other hand, the binary form, which accounts for only a small number of Carissimi's cantatas, represents nearly half of Luigi's and of Caproli's. This may be because more of Luigi's and Caproli's cantatas are ensembles, which for the most part tend to be binary pieces.

It is not possible to ascribe the invention of a form, or the consistent development of a peculiar stylistic feature, to Luigi or to any one of his contemporaries.[16] A chief reason for this, of course, is the difficulty of establishing any precise chronology across the entire cantata repertoire. But it seems, in addition, that the genre was so broadly based that no one individual of the period can be said to have shaped it decisively. Most of the practices we shall be discussing—e.g. that of setting certain verses of a strophe in aria style—are so common as to preclude specific identification with any one composer.

Although Luigi was not demonstrably an originator of forms, he reveals the various distinctive features of the musical designs he chose to work much as a sculptor frees the lines and curves of a figure imprisoned within his materials. The design is not a mere formal patterning of the surface, but a complete and complex organism. Eloquent bel canto passages, expressive arioso refrains, and dramatic recitatives are witnesses of Luigi's passionate feelings and fine sensibility. Interesting alternation of melismatic and syllabic divisions over an ostinato bass is but one manifestation of his ingenuity. Jagged broken lines, irregular phrases, juxtaposition of movement and immobility, contrast of metric units, continuous unfolding of the inner phrases with little repetition, long stretches of melody, interpolations of affective cries, sudden changes from one style of singing to another, and subtle variations in repeated cadences—all these testify to the fertility and to the poetic quality of Luigi's imagination.

In the tradition of the early Baroque monodists, the vocal line is usually intimately linked with the word, especially in matters of rhythm. There are, to be sure, instances where the textual values are inaccurately rendered in the musical setting—a glaring example is the beginning of the ternary cantata *Non mi lusingar* (ex. XXIV). (A collection of examples of whole cantatas or of extensive portions of them begins on p. 201. These examples are numbered with roman numerals; the short examples placed after p. 134 are numbered with arabic numerals.) This is but one obvious instance of the renewed ascendancy, in mid-seventeenth-century music, of the growing polarization between aria and recitative style. Such occasional lapses, it should be noted, are found only in aria movements and never in recitatives. They by no means imply a renunciation on Luigi's part of the spirit of the early monodic reforms. His commitment to the monodists' elusive ideal of "mirabili effetti" manifests itself in other ways. The highly ornamental and grandiose elements predominating in other artistic products of the time are alien to Luigi's cantatas; yet he shares to a remarkable degree the histrionic streak that so forcefully qualifies the Seicento as a whole. This makes itself repeatedly apparent—in concitato passages and in their sharp contrast with pathetic phrases, in dynamic affective skips, in changes of register, meter, tempo and movement, in dramatic pauses, and in the strong evocation of moods and sentiments suggested in the texts. The cantatas are innately human and poetic.

Although Luigi produced many fine laments and arie di più parti and contributed to the development of the unique larger forms of the chamber cantatas, leading the way to the extended cantatas of the latter half of the century, his primary achievement lies in the smaller cantatas. Luigi's main achievement is in the clarification of the principles of contrast and unity in the evolution of small musical forms. His cantatas in their own time were among the best known and most highly esteemed representatives of the genre. During the composer's lifetime they were sought after not only in the place of his activity, but in other musical and intellectual centers of Europe.[17]

Highest praise was accorded Luigi by contemporary writers and later ones, even into the next century.[18] A study of the music reveals that this estimation was well deserved.

Chapter 1

The Subject Matter of the Texts

The first part of this discussion treats of the "ariette corte," whose texts concern romantic love. They make up the greater number of the cantatas. A brief summary of the texts of the "arie di più parti" or extended canzonettas and of the laments follows. The cantatas that do not have to do with romantic love—a few ariettas and arie di più parti concerning moral conduct and the mortality of human life, and one arietta that pertains to a "sacred" subject, in that it speaks of the Holy Virgin and her Son— will concern us next, followed by comments on the remaining four cantatas, which are penitential laments. Some remarks on the texts' deeper meanings and a few observations pertaining to the poetic devices employed will conclude the chapter.

The singer of the cantata is almost without exception a lover, unidentified except for his sex. In the tradition of love poetry, he is a male in all but three of the "canzonette amorosi" or "ariette corte." One aspect of his personality is developed in the text: his attitude towards love. His decision for or against constancy and resignation, his willingness or reticence to serve—these form the core of his expressions. Either the lover is the devoted cavalier: responsible, noble, gallant—the traditional *cicisbeo*— or he is an egotistical pseudo-lover.

The love professed in the many ariette corte is not love that involves the whole person—heart, mind and body. It is, rather, a fashionable activity. Unlike the troubadours, the poets are not wholeheartedly convinced that the love of a woman is a virtue, and they distrust passionate love. One feels this distrust in the lack of force and truth in their expressions of love. Although the frequent exclamation "pene, pianti e sospiri" might suggest the involvement of the body, heart and mind-spirit, there is no real substance to the experience. The exterior poses, the gestures— languishing, weeping, sorrowing—are but an inferior level of the love- experience. One finds that the "falling-in-love" stage, the phase of symp- toms, is the theme of the texts, rather than the development and fulfillment of love. Only in the laments do we find lovers who are not merely courtiers, but truly lovers and tragic figures.

The basic concept of love, however, stated repeatedly and in diverse ways, is that love is service and an unsatiated longing for union with the beloved. It is the traditional psychic posture of the romantic lover: to be in love is to live in a fever, hoping but not expecting, wanting but not seeking, finding joy in the mere glance of the beloved, or in whatever guerdon her charity prompts her to bestow, but mostly in suffering itself. The lover sees his joy and peace centered in the beloved, whom he has vowed to serve, yet he does not consider the reciprocation of his love an essential part of his experience. He believes his severe torments an unquestionable necessity and, though he may request pity, he does not demand it or make it a requirement for his constancy.

The rhetorical paradox equating misery and death with joy and life is the main point of many texts; where it is not explicitly stated it is implied:

> Nel grave ardor ch'io sento,
> m'è riposo il penar, pace il tormento.
>
> —*Ahi, quante volte*

The lover pledges himself to eternal service, forfeiting his liberty. The "catena gradita," the "soave catene," and "cara servitù"—all mean love.[1] Again and again the lover asserts his "costanza," his "fermezza," no matter if the beloved disbelieves or deceives.

Destiny for the lover is "il morire" and "l'atroce martire." He is enticed by a beatuy that will torment him, but his heart hurries to the light of her beautiful face as a butterfly to the flame that will burn and destroy it. He nourishes his pains in the fire of his love.[2] In the face of this fate, his heart and soul continue obdurate. "Un amante ostinato," "un'anima ostinata," "un ostinato core"—this is the true lover unloved.

Such a one often despairs, yet he will not relinquish his love. The more he must suffer for it, the more precious becomes his treasure. Aware that he who serves has nothing to hope, the lover nevertheless urges his heart to suffer. Pains and torments are expected, welcomed and endured:

> Raddoppiatemi le pene!
>
> —*No, mio bene*

Is the love professed completely sincere? While declaring an abiding and insatiable love, the lovers show more concern for their state of being, their torments, their dread despair and anxiety; the assertions of constant faith are made with an overtone of vanity and self-appreciation. They play the lover because the role endows them with certain honor and prestige. Unrequited ardor is displayed in the form of a boast. The cries of anguish are pure histrionics. With a "lagrimoso ciglio" (*In questo duro*) the participants threaten to succumb to the throes of love-death. But neither love nor the beloved is of primary concern. From one moment to the next, they resolve to give up their passion in favor of their comfort:

> Ma poi meglio pensando e ripensando
> alla propria salute
> senza tante cadute
> stimò miglior partito amor penando.
> Quindi, fattosi accorto
> l'amante scaltro
> risolve andar a casa e non fare altro.

> —*Da perfida speranza*

Unconvinced of the "suffer and endure" concept of love, and doubtful of their gains in the involvement, the complaining lovers regret their commitment. They dwell on the beloved's cruelties and emphasize the hopelessness of their fate. Their songs are an endless catalogue of "lamenti," "pianti," "martiri," "tormenti," "catene," "sospiri," "dolori," "affani," "pene," and "lagrime." The cantata becomes "il flebil suon di giuste querele" (*Sognai, lasso*). Seldom owing to separation from the beloved, or sadness at her departure (*Deh, perche*; *Hor ch'io vivo*, and the laments), the cry of anguish is often a cry born of self-pity. Their fate is gloomy:

> Nulla strinse se non il suo tormento,
> le fortune d'amor sono di vento.

> —*V'è, v'è*

With some sarcasm a lover concludes:

> Ma corri quanto sai, speme amorosa,
> che chi segue beltà mai si riposa.

> —*Guardate dove va*

But only rarely do the complaints against the beauty's cruelty become invectives against women in general, or take the form of reproachful and offensive accusations (*Non piu viltà*, *Amor così*).

More sincere, perhaps, are the milder complaints. The faithful lover reproaches his beloved, he requests his rights or warns that, unless kindness and gratitude be shown him, he will not be enchained.[3] He speaks, for he hopes that:

> la lingua che parla ardita
> sa vincer la crudeltà.
>
> —*Un cor che*

Another group of texts represents spirited resolutions to break with love rather than complaints and protestations of love. They deride the conventional cries of anguish and sing in praise of freedom. Typically the lover resolves to harden his heart to the allurements of some beauty; he urges his heart to rid itself of grief and regain the liberty for which he longs. Although some of the lovers voice their resolutions with regret, others gloat over their new freedom and proclaim their joy:

> Dopo lungo penare
> tornato in libertà
> Amor mi disse "olà!
> ritorna a lagrimare
> se no che ti farò!"
> Io gli risposi, "otò!"
>
> —*Dopo lungo penare*

The basic concept of love is reaffirmed in these texts, for the lover's quarrel is with love as complete dedication and subordination; with love as servitude. He will have no more of chains and imprisonment.

The rebellious lovers, having regained their freedom, defend their position. They rebuke their hearts and hopes; they warn others and especially youth:

> Il languir per amor è l'esser matto!
>
> —*Chi d'amor sin ai capelli*

The experienced lover teaches that the wounds of love never heal, that the flower of life is lost in slavery to love. He warns of self-deception and he urges:

> Non amar tanto, no!
> Ama poco, ama poco!
>
> —*Se nell'arsura*[4]

The aria di più parti *Giusto così va detto* closes with a vigorous injunction:

> Le donne assai peggior son del carbone,
> questo o vi tinge, o scotta;
> ma quelle, o tutte o buone,
> han del carbon senza cangiar mai tempre
> solo una qualità: scottano sempre!

The most bitter of the lovers suggests unfaithfulness as a means of coping with the situation:

> Segui la fraude e non la fe, mio core!
>
> —*Deggio dunque*

And he resolves:

> Meglio al fine è tradir ch'esser tradito!
>
> —*Chi me credeva*

This, however, is an extreme point of view, and rarely expressed.

Conflict is the theme of another group of texts. The lovers see the weakness of hope and permit reason to convince them of hope's vanity. The conflict is between the Heart or Hope—which symbolizes the irrational, impulsive, emotional longing for love—and Reason, which sees Hope as dangerous and false. Reason speaks for liberty and against Love's enslavement; she wars against Hope, the flatterer and deceiver. But Reason almost always loses the battle. No matter that the lovers realize their self-deception; they silence Reason. They choose to abide by the rule of Love:

> Rendetevi, pensieri,
> non contrastate più
> Libertà non si speri;
> è destino al mio cor la servitù.
> No, non contrastate più!
>
> —*Rendetevi, pensieri*

Thought is not consistently represented as Hope's adversary, but in the tradition of the Provençal troubadour, Thought is inflamed by Love and becomes Hope's ally. Love gives the Heart battle through the thoughts that relentlessly torment it, urging constancy and long-suffering. The lovers react in various ways. One will have no more of this urging and begs to be permitted to release his pitiful sighs of torment. Another blames his thoughts for his slavery and, considering them his fiercest enemies, resolves to make a vigorous offensive against them.

This role of thoughts is part of the Petrarchan tradition In fact, in Luigi's *Dolenti pensieri miei, datevi pace*, the words "datevi pace" recall the opening of Petrarch's famous sonnet *Datemi pace*, which concerns the lover's conflict: "Guerra è 'l mio stato." In Sonnet XII of the Scottish poet Drummond of Hawthornden, so influenced by the Petrarchan tradition, the same theme appears: "Ah burning thoughts, now let me take some rest."[5] An ingenious text, *Infelici pensieri*, describes the allegiance of thoughts and hope by means of a sustained metaphor. It is the only cantata text known to me in which a funeral scene is enacted. Thoughts enter, the pallbearers of Hope. As they walk in the funeral procession they sing an elegy mourning Hope's death. The lover approaches them to ask for whom they mourn. On hearing of Hope's death he despairs with them. In bitterness they together accuse Woman's heart of tyranny. The lover then questions the pallbearers, asking whether Hope left an offspring. The thoughts reply that Hope expected the birth of Joy and Delight, but that they were stillborn. The lover grieves and despairs.

The lovers who would truly quarrel with love do not call upon thoughts and reason to act in their defense; they know that the only effective weapons against love are disdain and anger. Reason may instigate rebellion, but only disdain can stand against love's assaults (*Difenditi, amore*; *Armatevi di sdegno*).

The realistic side of Italian character is revealed in a number of texts. The lover's actions and sentiments, exemplary of the contemporary romantic attitude, are stated dispassionately. One text sets forth various paradoxes:

> Con amor e senza spene
> un bel niente mi mantiene!
> . . ..
> E se ben mi pasce d'aria
> mi banchetta col digiuno
> . . ..
> E 'l piacer che termin trova
> è sepolcro all'appetito.
> Solo il niente sempre ardito
> spirti[6] nutre entro le vene.
>
> —*Con amor*

The few texts in which the lover stands outside his experience and appraises it objectively reveal the awareness of all concerned that the laments, sighs, pains and torments are created by the lovers' imaginations and desires:

> Son tutte inventioni,
> son tutte canzoni,
> son vani pensieri,
> vapori leggieri
> del sangue che bolle.
> Chi vi crede è ben folle!
>
> —*Che sospiri, martiri*

An ingenious variation on the usual tearful complaint, Tenaglia's *Che volete ch'io canti*,[7] allows us to see into the mind of the singer as he decides how best to lament. He considers the value of his song in terms of its effect: "Will it produce results? Will it win her over to me?" Tenaglia's cantata is one of the few in which cantatas are mentioned. The example par excellence of this type is Cesti's *Aspettate*.[8] Another piece (which probably precedes Cesti's) containing references to the various types of cantatas by which lovers confess and protest their love is Luigi's aria di più parti *Noi siam tre donzellette* (see below, p. 17). In this piece we find typical ariette corte quoted within the cantata. In Cesti's piece the singer is the musician himself, a proud professional protesting the abuses of his art. In Luigi's cantata the singers are not the originators of the cantatas quoted, but the girls to whom the cantatas were sung.[9]

Music is mentioned in regard to its soothing, calming qualities in *Se dolente*, whereas in *Benche roca* the lover's lament, accompanied by the sound of the *cetra*, is sung to "il metro di dolore." This phrase seems to refer to the Greek "threnos" and its contemporary equivalent, the arioso lament. Its mention indicates the keen awareness of the distinctions among different rhythms, meters and modes of singing.

Undesirable effects of the love experience, or particular factors that crop up to mar its perfection, such as jealousy and deceit, are mentioned in few of the texts. One arietta, *Gelosia*, has jealousy as its theme. The lover expresses his longing to be rid of its poison. The other occurrences of this theme are in the arie di più parti *Mostro d'ali* and *Animi voi*, the latter famous in its day. One other cantata mentions the fact that the particular lover is afflicted by jealousy: the duo *Compatite*, in which jealousy is likened to ice in its effect upon a burning heart, a typical emblematic image.

Perfidy, the other undesirable element in human love relationships, is described as an invasive growth, wholly unnatural to love. The text *Chi non sa* is permeated with words referring to it: "fingere," "mescherato," "frodi," "mentire." Finally the point is made: Cupid is a naked child, without deceit. Warnings against perfidy also occur in *Così va*, where examples of its evil are cited from mythology.

Few texts show the lover affirming the hope of joy in love:

> E chi sa ch'un giorno anch'io
> in amor non sia felice?
>
> —*A me stesso*

Rare is the lover who invites love in without fear of deceit or thought of suffering. Rare is he who asserts that perseverance brings rewards. A particular mental attitude emerges from the few texts that exhort courage and audacity: opportunities for enjoyment go to those who are willing to take the chance. As the texts put it:

> Se non ami, non godi!
>
> —*Libertà, ragion*
>
> Nulla ottiene già mai chi nulla tenta.
>
> —*Tenti e ardisca*
>
> Chi più volte s'arrischia è alfin beato.
>
> —*Tornate, o miei sospiri*

Even in the rare texts that describe a woman's view diverse attitudes are expressed. Answering the complaints of her lover, a girl beseeches him to be courteous and kind, promising that his patience will be rewarded (*Fanciulla son'io*).[10] With a rare affirmation of the good involved in being in love, Corilla learns that love is not a snake that bites but that love is joy (*Io ero pargoletta*).[11] Quite another attitude is expressed by a jilted and humiliated woman. She assumes a haughty mien and reminds all that she holds many loving hearts prisoner (*Frena i pianti*). Expressing the cautious view, but in a spirited manner, the text of *Fanciulle tenete* warns women to be wary of the promises and compliments of men. They are not to be trusted!

Unlike other poetry of the time, the cantata texts avoid mention of the beloved's physical attributes—the exceptions being the eyes, which are often referred to and are the central theme of several texts, and, less often, the mouth. One aria di più parti closes with a hyberbolic eulogy extolling the beauty of Filli's eyes: Febo, Cintia and Apollo must cede to their splendor.[12] But the beauty of the beloved is not mentioned as often in praise as it is in complaint. The texts focus on the harshness the beautiful eyes and mouth are capable of and on the suffering they can inflict.

Frequently the poets refer to the beloved's eyes with the traditional images of light, whereby the eyes represent the spirit, the soul. But these references do not have the meaning that they have in the poetry of the *stilnovisti*. The lady is not seen as a species of heavenly spirit. She is not a Beatrice that moves the lover's soul upward through her gentleness and beauty. Perhaps the importance of the beloved's eyes may be symbolic of the lover's nostalgia for a spiritual relationship. The eyes described, however, are often black, in the tradition of the Renaissance madrigal. Since black is the absence of light, the element of spirit may be ruled out in favor of association with passionate, sensual love.

Yet little mention is made of caresses and embraces; the physical aspect of love is hinted at in only two texts (*Tu giuri; La bella per cui son cieco*) and then in a jesting manner, in reference to love as a game, as parrying in a duel. The lover boldly but playfully reproaches his lady, who has sworn that her heart is his, for not permitting him to touch it. Luigi did not compose for those who favored the "lascivi," one of the types of cantatas Cesti mentions in *Aspettate*. We know that his cantatas were sung in the *saloni* of the elite, before audiences of high churchmen and nobles, or from below the balconies of ladies' residences.[13] The physical element would be incongruous and indelicate.

Although the arie di più parti treat the same subjects as the ariette corte—the amorous patterns are the same—there is a frequent and developed use of dialogue, dreams, fantasies, and scene-complexes that is uncharacteristic of the ariette corte. In a few cantatas the singers are the shepherds of Aminta and Filandro, but ususally they are anonymous lovers. In the ariette corte the beloved is rarely mentioned by name, while in the arie di più parti she is frequently identified. Filli appears more than Lilla, Clori, Corilla, Lucinda and Amarilli. Although the names recall the pastoral tradition, it is not important in the poetry of Luigi's cantatas.

The same personifications and similes found in the ariette corte are used in the longer cantatas. Thought, Reason and Hope are in constant dialogue with the lover, inciting him, tormenting him, or agreeing with his inclinations. In one rare humorous cantata (*E che pensi*) the lover interrogates his heart in a teasing manner, meaning thus to demonstrate the constancy of his faith.

One of the interesting dialogues, and the longest of the arie di più parti, *Noi siam tre donzellette*, is a developed miniature scena. Three "donzellette" are out walking in the countryside; they stop to exchange stories about their amorous involvements, commenting, not without a bit of mockery, upon the various ways the young men speak and sing to them. They successfully convey the histrionic quality of their professed lovers' confessions of love.

This cantata is a catalogue of typical ariettas. The text, under the guise of women's chatter, is an objective, unemotional review of the exaggerated protestations of passionate love common in the cantatas and probably representative of the declarations of contemporary lovers.

Unlike the lovers mocked by the "donzellette"—those whose cries are usually an uncontrolled display of a simulated state of soul—the protagonist of the laments feels genuine emotion. Hers is a controlled display of a sincere state of soul. The laments also involve conflict, inner struggle, and turmoil, whereas the canzonettas more usually concentrate on a single emotion.

The basic theme of the lament texts is separation from the beloved: separation through death or departure, separation through betrayal or abandonment. Most of the laments are the desperate cries of women whose love has been betrayed or is unrequited (*Quando Florinda*, *Erminia*, *Tra romite*, *All'hor*, *Con occhi*, *Sparsa il crine*).[14] Several of the cantatas are laments for the death or the departure of a faithful beloved (*Un ferito*, *Correa*, *Hora ch'ad eclissar*). Understandably, laments by men are rare. Unrequited love is the cause of the lament of the anonymous shepherd in *Orrida e solitaria*. Arione sings his lament in protest of his own imminent death as he is threatened by avaricious sailors (*Al soave*). Two brothers doomed to die sing their farewell to mother and wife in *Rugge*. The unusual cantata *Ravvolse il volo* is sung by Cupid and its theme is Cupid's desire for vindication, but it contains within it the death song of a dying lover. Cecco sings of unrequited love (*Sotto l'ombra*); his lament, however, is exploited for parodistic purposes.

Pairs of lovers are involved in some of the cantatas—*Tra romite*: Olimpia and Bireno; *Pur è ver*: Antony and Cleopatra; *Erminia*: Erminia and Tancredi; *Dentro negra foresta*: Armida and Rinaldo; *All'hor*: Alcide and Deianira; *Rugge quasi leon*: Baiazet and Daraida; *Correa*: Masaniello and Marinetta; and *Un ferito*: Gustavus Adolphus and his queen—yet these are all for a single voice and there is no dialogue. Mutual love is not the central theme; the tragic separation that divides the lovers and the anguish this causes are the subjects of the laments.

Unlike his Neapolitan compatriot and contemporary Orazio Michi, whose cantatas are almost exclusively settings of texts known as "spirituali' and "morali"—texts on sacred subjects and texts critical of the licentiousness of the times—Luigi set but 14 such texts (as opposed to hundreds of poems on love).[15] Among the ariette corte there are seven texts that do not treat of love; among the arie di più parti, three; and in the group of laments and recitatives, there are four.

A single cantata, *Diva, tu*, a binary piece, is a prayer to the Virgin that she intercede before her divine Son. Three more of the binary pieces, *Chi desia*, *Acuto gelo*, and *Ingordo human desio*, urge the abandonment of human affections and mundane pleasures, and a conversion of soul. A ternary piece, *Mortale, che pensi*, reminds mortals that human triumphs are ephemeral. The complex rondo *Ferma Giove*, whose theme is the evil of avarice, warns that gold will not satisfy human hearts, but that desire for it will lead to loss of peace and sanity. *Presso un ruscel*, an aria di più parti, concludes with an amonition:

> Apprendete, o viventi,
> a non fidarvi dell'età fugace.
> Il tempo ch'è fallace
> secoli mostrerà, ma son momenti.
> La vita di cui l'huom non si franca
> è un no che corre et un seren che manca.[16]

The theme is repeated in two recurring verses of the ensemble *Piangea l'aurora*:

> Nulla qua giù diletta e dura.
> . . ..
> Cosa bella mortale passa e non dura.

The theme of the mortality of human beauty is prominent in the cantata literature.[17] "Bellezza caduca"[18] is the subject of *Spuntava un dì* (*I* Bc, Q43, f.98), a cantata of five parts with a refrain almost identical to that of *Piangea*:

> Ma che pro? . . .
> Cosa bella qua giù passa e non dura!

In the Magdalene laments and the "Peccator pentito" cantatas, the same theme reappears. The Magdalene and the sinner confess their attachment to self and to the world. The Magdalene denounces her body:

> Io cadavero vile, io verme immondo!

> —*O grotto, o speco*

And the penitent accuses himself:

> Sol'io cadavero immondo
> . . ..
> Sol'io putrido vermo!

> —*Nel dì*

Magdalene describes her beauty:

> Hor'è tutto fetor, vermi et horrore
> . . ..
> questa vana beltade.

> —*O grotto, o speco*

and inculpates it with the death of Christ:

> . . . della mia bellezza
> il fasto, l'alterezza
> a par degl'uccisori, ucciso t'hanno.

> —*Pender non prima*

Of the three remaining short texts by Luigi that do not speak of love, two present a trend of thought contrary to the one spoken of above. The awareness of the perishable quality of human beauty and youth, as much present in these pieces as in the others, inspires an entirely different attitude. The two texts *Come tosto* and *Il cor mi dice* advocate a Cyrenaic hedonism, a surrender of the spirit to the here and now. Related to these texts by its negative tone, *Chi cercando* is a bitter complaint against the many troubles of the world and a pessimistic observation that little good exists.

The four penitential cantatas composed by Luigi—*Pender non prima*, *O grotta, o speco*, *Nel dì*, and *In solitario speco*—are personal confessions of guilt; they are public declarations of individual unworthiness, and are subjective and emotional in tone. The other "spirituali" and "morali" described above are, on the other hand, impersonal and essentially didactic.

In structure and mode of expression the penitential cantatas belong to the genre of laments. The protagonist in the first two mentioned is the Magdalene; in the others, an anonymous penitent. These passionate and sorrowful figures who represent the conflict of worldliness and spirituality were favorite subjects of the art of the Counter-Reformation. The texts that develop the emotional and theatrical possibilities of "la bella peccatrice" and the "peccator pentito" manifest a Baroque spirituality. Emphasis is on "gli affetti."

The tearful confession and the conflict of conversion are not truly religious. The poets treat the subject with a purely emotional sensitivity, and thus create superficial rather than profound feelings. The Magdalene's cries could be those of the loving Erminia; a personal, subjective quality dominates. The Magdalene of the cantatas is a pathetic figure. One need only see Carlo Dolci's portrait of her to realize the Magdalene's identification with languishing lovers.[19]

Two contrafacta, in fact, prove this association. In the cantata repertory the contrafactum is extremely rare. The two known to me occur with the laments of the Queen of Sweden (Luigi's *Un ferito cavaliero*) and Arianna (Monteverdi's *Lasciatemi morire* in *I* Bc, Q 43), pieces that were well known in their day. Both are extant with texts in which the Magdalene takes the place of the original protagonists. In each case the reviser did not rework the text, but tried to adapt it by changing words here and there. In the contrafacta the Magdalene appears more disordered and theatrical than dramatic; her sorrow seems hysterical.

Although the travesty of Luigi's *Un ferito cavaliero* is unsuccessful artistically—a look at the whole proves that its reasons for being are of an extrinsic nature[20]—it is a successful example of Seicento "ingegno." This Baroque predilection for the ingenious is evident in the transformation of the opening couplet:

> Ferito un cavalier
> di polve, di sudor, di sangue asperso

into:

> Un allato messaggiero
> da pietà, da stupor, da doglia oppresso.

The melancholy quality that permeates so many of the cantatas depends in part on a strong tendency in the texts towards resignation. A feeling of fatality or defeat runs as an undercurrent through the cantatas. Two conventional exclamations, which occur so frequently as to require attention, sum up this feeling: "Così va!" and "Ma che pro?"[21] The final verse or couplet of many cantatas[22] expresses the hopelessness conveyed at the close of *Tutto cinto*:

> . . . così va,
> sempre in peggio li torna il bel che fa.

In truth, love and deep involvement cause fruitful suffering, but in the poetry of the cantatas suffering seems to bear no fruit. Hence despair often results.

"Misera, ma che pro?"[23] The question receives no answer. Personality and destiny are immutable. Resignation is the enervating, paralyzing attitude that no courage rises to overcome. The words of the narrator in *Rugge quasi leon*:

> . . . Ma che pro,
> se nel tiranno reo pietà non è?

might be those of the Italians of the time, a people politically fragmented, suffering poverty, lorded over by haughty nobles and by foreigners; a society fallen into spiritual misery, whose religious feelings, especially in the upper classes, tended to be crystallized in exterior forms.

It is this poverty of spirit that lies at the root of Cecco's observation when he suddenly ceases calling to his friends and relatives for help. He exclaims:

> Ma . . . che vaneggio!
> Ah, che non son le genti d'oggi si matte
> che voglin qui fra noi
> mettersi a grattar rogna o pelar gatte
> e quastar per quei d'altri i fatti suoi.
>
> —*Sotto l'ombra*

Cecco is aware of the tendency of his people to concentrate on their personal interests, avoiding the problems of others.

Fear of becoming involved, fear of risking one's personal security, is also the source of Marinetta's unheeded advice:

> Quante volte ti dissi,
> marito mio, bada alli fatti tuoi!
> . . . .
> Quante volte ti dissi
> loca la lingua, Aniello!
>
> —*Correa l'ottavo giorno*[24]

The prevalent attitude seems to be: Protect yourself!

The same deep-rooted mental precautions and diffidence create the poverty of spirit that lies behind the fear of real relationships, the fear of risk that produces the prevailing concept of love. The metaphor in *Sovra un lido* conveys the point of the matter: falling in love is like going out from a safe port onto a smiling and inviting sea, which suddenly becomes stormy and treacherously drowns those who trusted it. "Ma che pro l'uscir dal lido?" wonders the lover.

Finally, the exclamation "Ma che pro?" is associated with a deep tragic sense of the immutability of death and the realization of the ineffectiveness of anger and vengeance towards men of violence. Interrupting her cries of vengeance, Masaniello's widow cries:

> Misera, ma che pro,
> se non per questo ritornar in vita
> la vita mia vedrò?
>
> —*Correa l'ottavo giorno*

And thus the Queen of Sweden's final cry begins:

> Misera, ma che pro?
> Per questo il mio Signor già non vivrà.
>
> —*Un ferito cavaliero*

Evidence of the significance of the two exclamations is given by the particular musical settings. In *De la vita* the first words of the refrain finale "così va" are set off as a typical introductory motto. In the ostinato section of *Tutto cinto*, "così va, così va" is placed in relief—silence precedes and follows the short, severe statement. The ostinato pattern drops for the first time to the low register (on its tenth repetition), and returns to the upper register after this phrase. Only at the close does it fall again. The musical setting intensifies the feeling of hopelessness (ex. 1).

The Phrygian cadence, typically associated with rhetorical questions that elicit no answer and also with feelings of despair, sets off "Ma che pro?" in *E che cantar*. The descending skip of the diminished fifth, sparingly employed in the cantatas and always for effective expression, qualifies the exclamation in Tenaglia's *Che ti resta* and in the anonymous *Correa l'ottava giorno*. In the latter a fine harmonic juxtaposition sets the words off as the opening of a new section (ex. 2).

A dramatic pause with a fermata noted over the barline follows "Ma, che mi giova, o Dio!" (a variant exclamation), which begins with a silence and an ascending octave skip in the opening of the third recitative of Luigi's *Lasciate ch'io ritorni*.

"Ma che pro? Si pugna invano!"—thus begin the second and third statements of the refrain of *Con amor si pugna*. The change in the text from the original "Con amor" to "Ma che pro?" is marked in the music by an appropriate musical change that sets off the passionate exclamation. The repeated Phrygian cadence, the syncopated rhythms, and the final affective fall of the diminished fifth interpret the words (ex. 3).

Other psychic postures are revealed in the gnomic verses that so frequently conclude the binary ariettas and the arie di più parti and also appear in the other cantatas. Usually the contents of these verses are not universal in application, but are directed to a group of people who have the same limited concerns as the singer. They advise mistrust of the cleverness of others, mistrust of the motives of others, they warn of betrayal and deception, they urge avoidance of what may be detrimental to personal pleasure and comfort:

> Chi vuol esser costante è alfin tradito!
>
> —*Chi mi credeva*
>
> Son le gioie d'amor fatte per gl'empi!
>
> —*Deggio dunque*
>
> Chi ritorna ad amar ama la morte!
>
> —*Misero cor*

Another trend that the prevalent use of these gnomic statements points to is that of "concettismo"—a tendency to conceptualize, to rationalize, and even moralize the aspects of the situation. Often, the verse precisely states the gist of the entire poem:

> Chi fortuna non ha, goder non può!
>
> —*A la rota*
>
> Una fe nobile perir non può!
>
> —*Mentre sorge*
>
> Chi non ama in eterno adora poco!
>
> —*No, mio bene*
>
> In amor chi non prova il pregar non sa concedere!
>
> —*Sempre dunque*
>
> Chi non vuol penar non ha costanza!
>
> —*Io mi glorio*

Although it seems that the closing aphorism sums up the "truth" or moral value that the poem implies, it may be that the rest of the text depends on it for its substance. It is possible that the text is composed with the closing conceit as point of departure. In this case, the body of the text serves to illustrate the epigrammatic point. This is suggested in the rondos, where the first member of the cantata, the refrain, is a gnomic saying or an impersonal and synthesizing comment. The proleptic announcement of the final gnomic statement of the aria di più parti *Pur è ver* at its outset also indicates this possible leading function of the concetto.

The subject and its mood determine the choice of poetic devices. One salient technique, a marinismo,[25] is the use of catalogues. Not having the taste for conciseness, the poets use pleonasms. Avoiding the pregnant word, they distend their thought in many words. Although the catalogue is heavy, it may have a quality of dynamic rigidity, which at its level creates an effect similar to that which the ostinato and musical sequence produce. The catalogue usually occurs at the beginning of the text, (*A i sospiri, al dolore, a i tormenti, al penare*; *Pensoso, afflitto, irresoluto e solo*; and *A la rota, a la benda, al biondo crine, al volto*. (For example, see Thematic Index I, no.248.) In the laments, however, the device is used internally, as in the last part of Arione's lament, where it occurs twice with theatrical emphasis:

O pianti, o doglie, o pene!

—Al soave

When it occurs in these longer cantatas, the catalogue usually marks the beginning of an inner section.

A quality of bravura is inherent in the catalogue as it is in the other literary devices: oxymoron, paradox, extended metaphor, hyberbole. The choice of ingenious and unusual ways of expression is an aspect of the tendency towards display of emotional aggressiveness.

By juxtaposition of contrary images, a simple fact is stated in two opposing ways:

Tu dal duol cavi contenti,
io godendo peno assai.

—Farfalletta che ten vai

Sente vana gloria
delle sue glorie vane.

—Tra montagne

E miseria d'un core anche la vita.
E delitia d'un core anche la morte.

—*O gradita libertà*

La vita di cui l'huom non si franca
e un no che corre et un seren che manca.

—*Presso un ruscel*

As in the catalogue, there is a seeming change with no change at all. Opposing images are combined in terse descriptive phrases:

In sepolcro vital

—*Farfalletta*

Ti confesso piangendo il noto arcano

—*In solitario*

Così m'ha fatto amore:
un argo cieco et un gelato ardore!

—*Un tiranno di foco*

Of all the devices the paradox occurs most frequently and it usually comes at the close of the cantatas. Among the many examples are the following final verses:[26]

Che fra 'l duolo e 'l tormento
moro per colei lieto e contento.

—*Horche fra l'ombre*

Passando hore per anni, anni per hore.

—*Tra montagne*

Il mio cor sol provò
un si che dice no.

—*Amanti, piangete*

And within the long cantata *Tutto cinto*, the tormented lover asks:

Hor come fia ch'io possa viver
tra duo contrar che son d'accordo?

Even in the passionate recitatives of the laments the impersonal paradox crops up, somewhat cool and objective in the midst of emotional cries. In the third recitative of *Erminia*, for example, the couplet:

> Ch'un infelice core
> cessa sol di morir all'hor che more.

could serve as conclusion for many an arietta.

In texts inherently hyberbolic in spirit, where even the previously mentioned devices are used with hyberbolic effect, the use of the hyperbole as a figure of speech in the Petrarchan tradition is a hallmark. An example:

> E godrò di perder poi
> non sol'una, mille vite!
>
> —*Luci mie*

Personification occurs frequently—Love, Hope, Fortune, Thought, Heart—these consistently speak, engage in dialogues, appear in dreams. As I have already shown, frequent quarrels between the Heart and Thought are generally described in metaphors. In *Tutto cinto*, a popular mode of expression makes the metaphor quite spirited:

> Che ei (il core) d'uscir non ardisce
> perche de miei pensier qualche brigata teme.

Two interesting texts in which personification is combined with metaphor and sustained throughout are the arie di più parti *Chi batte il mio core* and *Infelici pensieri*. (The latter is discussed above, p. 14.) In *Chi batte* Love knocks at a heart's door, but the heart isn't home; she is out looking for a vain hope. Love enters by force through the eyes. Agitation follows. There is general concern about what the heart will do when she returns. In *S'era alquanto* the metaphor that accompanies the personification of the heart is truly "Baroque." The heart is awakened by the sounds of the chains of love attached to its feet.

A related rhetorical device, that occurs more frequently in the longer than in the shorter cantatas, is metonymy—the naming of mythological figures in place of what they symbolize: Cupido and Venere—love; Febo the archer—the sun; Ausonia the nymph—Italy; Citherea—the moon; and Bromio—wine.

The traditional themes of Sleep and Night also figure in the poetry of the cantatas. They appear with various symbolic meanings. In some texts sleep is respite from love's torments; it brings solace to the lover. Similarly, night brings peace; it announces joyful oblivion.[27] But in other texts, sleep increases the lover's pain. Visions of the beloved cause him greater grief. "Mille imagini false in sogno" torment him. Sleep brings no relief, but the flames in the lover's heart burn more ardently. Night is separation from the beloved who is Light.[28]

Fortune, another conventional theme of Seicento poetry, is frequently mentioned in the texts, appearing as a protagonist in the long cantata *A la rota*. Preoccupation with her unchallenged power is a manifestation of strong passive and pessimistic tendencies—tendencies such as produce the exclamations "Ma che pro?" and "Così va!" The attitude is that Man is not master of his circumstances.

One of the most prominent attributes of a great number of cantata texts is the refrain. The final hendecasyllable of a binary arietta, the reprise of a rounded binary strophe, the refrain quatrain of the rondo, and the refrain of a lament, all contain within them the central idea or the basic "affetto" of the text. A catalogue of these verses would define and document the prevalent attitudes towards love and life as they are expressed in the cantatas.

Although it is occasionally an impersonal statement of fact, the recurrent concluding verse of the strophic binary ariettas is more often an affective exclamation. It is an exhortation, a plea, an admonition, a command, a strong assertion, or a resolution to keep faith or never to love again. Only a few are outbursts of grief, or of deep longing for an unobtainable objective:

Viva la servitù!	—*A i sospiri*
Su, su, dunque, all'armi!	—*Viemmi, o sdegno*
Struggesi, fuggesi il gelo d'asprezza al sole della bellezza!	—*Che non puote*
Taci, lingua, taci, amor lo sa!	—*A qual dardo*
Ama poco, ama poco!	—*Se nell'arsura*
Filli, non chiedo amor, chiedo pietà!	—*Filli, non penso*
Lasciami, gelosia!	—*Gelosia*
Ahime, gridando e replicando, ahi, ahi, ahi!	—*Ahi, dunque*
Non amo più, no!	—*Piansi già*
No no, amerò, seguirò la beltà!	—*Poiche mancò*

The rondo refrains and rounded binary reprises are also expressive verses: exhortations, commands, rhetorical questions and pleas:[29]

Defendi, mio core, l'entrata ad amore!

Sospiri, su, su!

Fanciulla son' io, ch'amare non so,
Ahi, ahi, che mi morirò!

Adorate mie catene,
deh d'affligermi lasciate
horche gita e via la speme,
a che più mi tormentate?

E chi non v'ameria,
pupilluccie amorose,
mentre tanto pietose
voi sete a l'alma mia?
E chi non v'ameria?

Non ha core, no,
non ha vita chi non apprezza
gl'alti pregi de la bellezza!

—*Sopra conca*

Voglio precipitarmi!

—*Da perfida*

But among them there are also impersonal summations and didactic statements:

Chi non ha speranza alcuna
che lusinghi il suo pensiero
poco teme la fortuna!

Chi non sa fingere, goder non sa!

Cosí va, dice il mio core,
in amore chi più serve manco fa!

Tra montagne di foco
romito vive il core
passando hore per anni, anni per hore!

Whether they are gnomic verses or affective utterances, the refrains are all exclamations and it is this fervent quality of expression that makes their recurrence so appropriate.

The refrain of a lament is an exclamation or an exhortation; it is a plea, a cry for mercy, or an expression of hopeless grief. It is always intensely affective and its recurrence is a psychological necessity. For example:

Che fai, che pensi, ohime, misera mori!

—*Quando Florinda*

The return of the refrain verse or verses is usually well motivated and reasonably convincing. The expression is emphatic and agressive; the recurrence reinforces these qualities.

The amatory patterns repeated in the texts recall the fervor of *fin amor* and the concept of service that is its basis,[30] but the sentiments of the *fin amant* are expressed with an exaggeration that belies their sincerity. The poets do not express the poetic exaltation, the joy and adoration of the *courtois*, but voice pessimism. The lovers of the cantatas are not absorbed in service, in the exaltation of beauty, in the vital relationship of man and woman, but rather in their own psychic conflicts.

Although the protestations of love are those of romantic passion, repeatedly we find assertions that love is a dangerous and unsettling experience. Wholehearted dedication is abnegated in this classic view of love.[31] Perhaps the inherent histrionic quality of the texts is due to the conflict between the two points of view. The poet wants to appear totally involved and as a result he exaggerates.

One of Luigi's cantatas frankly admits the poets' concern with appearance. The lover beseeches his lady in an original manner.

> Non mi fate mentire,
> ho già detto a ciascun che voi m'amate.
> Se poi vi rimutate,
> mi vedrete morire.
> Non mi fate mentire!
> Troppo sarei dolente,
> che direbbe la gente?
> Riderebbe ciascun del mio martire.
> Non mi fate mentire!

The desire to cut a good figure—in this the poem is completely sincere. The appearance must be right.

Artificiality is the primary trait of this poetry and it is real, just as the theater is real.

Chapter 2

Ariette Corte: General Formal and Stylistic Traits

The four overall formal designs found in the ariette corte—binary, rounded binary, ternary and rondo—are essentially the product of differing repetition and recapitulation schemes, not of differing musical or textual substance. With few exceptions[1] the cantatas of these four groups are composed of two units that are clearly differentiated both textually and musically. The first units of the four formal types share a large number of characteristics in common as against a small number of characteristics that are not so shared; likewise the second units, which are readily distinguishable from the first units. In almost all cases, the traits that are not held in common pertain to overall formal differences.

The similarities and differences among the four formal types will be set forth in this chapter. Those features, both textual and musical, that are independent of the overall formal differences will be described in detail. In the subsequent sections I will review the traits that differentiate one group from the others, show a few of the unusual realizations of the basic forms, and summarize the essential features of each group.

The Repetition and Recapitulation Schemes. The binary and rounded binary cantatas are two-part designs. In the binary the first unit is generally repeated before it is followed by the second unit, but in the rounded binary there is usually no repetition of the first unit—the second unit immediately follows it. A distinguishing mark of the rounded binary design is the recapitulation of part of the first unit at the close of the second; the segment that is quoted (both words and music) is usually the concluding passage, but in a few cases it is the opening phrase. The two units of the simple binary are not usually related musically or textually by the recurrence of any portion of the first unit in the second.

The ternary pattern consists of the two units sung in succession, and a reprise of the first unit with its original text. The rondo is an expansion of this design. It requires at least two recurrences of the first unit with its original text. Between these recurrences the second unit is heard with new text, or less frequently a third unit, with new music and text.[2] With each letter representing a unit, upper case signifying retention of the original text and lower case signifying new text, the respective patterns are: Ternary: A b A, Rondo: A b A b A or A b A c A.

Strophic repetition, which is the recurrence of one or both musical units with a new text that retains the rhyme and metric schemes of the first set of verses, is very frequent in the binary and rounded binary cantatas, and most common in the rondos. Relatively few ternary cantatas are strophically repeated. There are two kinds of strophic repetition: the entire cantata is repeated with new text, or only the second unit recurs with new text. The first kind of strophic design is typical of all the binary and ternary cantatas, but is characteristic of only a minority of the rounded binary. The second kind is typical of all the rondos of two units and of the majority of the rounded binary. The pattern of repetition in these rounded binary cantatas is quite different from that of the rondo pattern. Whereas the second unit of the rondo and its strophic repetition are separated by the recurrence of the rondo refrain, those of the rounded binary are heard in succession, and the concluding passage, which is quoted from the first unit, does not incur textual change. With "a" representing the body of the first unit; "B," its conclusion and "c," the second unit, this rounded binary pattern is: aB/ cB/ cB. Texts of the strophic binary, rounded binary, ternary and rondo cantatas are quoted below, pp. 41-42, 34-35, 42-44, respectively.

Strophic variation, in the relatively few instances where Luigi employs it, is not a means of formal expansion—in the sense of extending the cantata significantly beyond the length achieved by simple strophic repetition. As in earlier monodic music, strophic variation permits a more precise declamation of the verses of the second and subsequent stanzas and the interpretation of particular words with affective musical gestures. Strophic variation embellishes the repeated units of a given form; it is not a form in itself. The procedures of variation are the same in all the formal types and are discussed below, pp. 79-81.

Text Structure. In general the two units of all four cantata types are unequal in number of verses—the second unit is normally longer than the first. However, among the binary cantata texts, there is a large minority whose two units are composed of the same number of verses[3]—usually four—or whose second unit is shorter than the first.[4] In fact, only among the binary texts do we find second units that are no longer than a couplet. This characteristic probably accounts for the fact that there is more text repetition at the close of a binary cantata than anywhere else in the ariette corte. The binary texts are poems from six to ten verses long; a quatrain often forms either of the units and, as mentioned, sometimes both.[5] The texts of the other three groups are generally longer than the typical binary text and average 13 verses. The quatrain is nowhere as prevalent in these texts as it is in the binary.

First unit rhyme patterns that prevail in all the cantata texts are abba and abab, and in the rounded binary, ternary and rondo texts, also AbbaA.[6] Recurring overall rhyme patterns are few and form only a small minority of the texts of each type. Of those found in the binary cantatas the only prevalent ones are abba cc and abab ccdd, each forming the design of eight cantatas. In the rounded binary, ternary and rondo cantatas, there is only one pattern that recurs: AbbaA cddcceea (with A recapitulated at the close of the rounded binary second unit).

The recapitulation of the introductory verse of a unit at its close, known as the envelope design, is characteristic of first units only. It is a hallmark of the rounded binary cantatas—16 of the 19 cantatas of this group begin with it—and occurs in a large minority of ternary and rondo texts, but is rare in the binary texts.[7] This design is not an arbitrary one determined by the composer, but it is an integral part of the poetic scheme. Proof of this is the number of texts found among Giovanni Lotti's published poems "per musica" (cf. Introduction, note 12) that begin with a short strophe whose last verse is the same as the opening one.

Also found in this collection of seventeenth-century poetry are rounded binary texts like those composed by Luigi. In these poems the first verse recurs not only at the close of the first unit, but also at the close of the second. Another type of verse recurrence is characteristic of many of the simple binary texts of two or more strophes.[8] Here the final verse or couplet of the original second unit recurs in each of the subsequent strophes in the same place.[9] With "a" representing the first unit; "b," the first segment of the second; "c," the concluding segment of the second, and upper case, recurrence of both music and text, the design is: a /bC // a / bC // a / bC //. Similar to this refrain pattern is that of the abbreviated strophic rounded binary texts: aB / cB // cB // (cf. above, p. 32).

The binary and rounded binary texts share another trait in that both conclude with a rhyming couplet; but in the rounded binary texts, the final verse is recalled from the first unit. If this reprise verse were omitted, the rounded binary text would be virtually indistinguishable from the ternary and rondo texts. Its second unit would end with a verse rhyming with the opening verse of the first unit—a trait of nearly all ternary and rondo texts. In fact, there is sufficient similarity between rounded binary, ternary and rondo texts that one text may be set in any of three ways— the texts of *Ohime, madre, aita*, *Difenditi, amore*, and *Difenditi, o core* are examples in point. The first was set by Luigi as a rounded binary cantata and by Mario Savioni as a rondo. Luigi omitted the recurrence of the first unit as refrain, recapitulating only its first verse at the close of each of the strophes of the second unit. Savioni, on the other hand, used the first unit as a rondo refrain, recapitulating it intact after each of the strophes:[10]

Luigi's version:

First unit:

  Ohime, madre, aita, aita!
  Già nel cor mi sento un foco
  che non visto a poco a poco
  mi vuol togliere la vita.
  Ohime, madre, aita, aita!

Second unit:

  Sotto l'arco d'un bel ciglio
  io non so se fusse amore;
  splender viddi un vivo ardore
  che raddoppia il mio periglio.
  Non è tempo di consiglio
  chiede aiuto il mio tormento.
  Io già moro, io già mi sento
  l'alma tutta incenerita.

Closing verse:

  Ohime, madre, aita, aita!

  Ohime, madre, aita, aita!
  Già nel cor mi sento un foco
  che non visto a poco a poco
  mi vuol togliere la vita.
  Ohime, madre, aita, aita!

Second unit repeated:

  Se penando io già languisco,
  se quegl'occhi il cor m'han tolto,
  giurerei ch'entro quel volto
  esser chiuso un basilisco.
  Di mirar più non ardisco
  la cagione de miei quai,
  ch'al fulgor di quei bei rai
  già la morte il ciel m'addita.

Closing verse:

  Ohime, madrè, aita, aita!

  Ohime, madre, aita, aita!
  Già nel cor mi sento un foco
  che non visto a poco a poco
  mi vuol togliere la vita.
  Ohime, madre, aita, aita!

Mario's version:

Rondo refrain:

Rondo strophe:

Closing verse:

Rondo refrain:

Rondo strophe repeated:

Closing verse:

Rondo refrain:

The two *Difenditi* texts, both set by Luigi, were probably derived by him from one poem. Although one is a strophic rounded binary cantata and the other a nonstrophic ternary, the texts have the same second unit. The first units are not identical, but they have the same number of verses, the same metric and rhyme patterns and are constructed as stanzas for a strophic setting—one can be substituted for the other:

Rounded binary
First unit:

> Difenditi, amore!
> Per foco di sdegno
> si perde il tuo regno,
> s'estingue il tuo ardore.
> Difenditi, amore!

Ternary reprise:

> Difenditi, o core!
> Per lampo fugace
> si perde la pace,
> s'estingue il tuo ardore.
> Difenditi, amore!

Second unit:

Ternary reprise:

> Con onda homicida
> di pianto di sangue,
> chi misero langue
> a guerra ti sfida.
> Le voci, le strida,
> gl'affanni, i lamenti
> son fulmini ardenti
> d'un alma che more.

Closing verse:

> Difenditi, amore!

Ternary reprise:

> Difenditi, o core!
> Per lampo fugace
> si perde la pace,
> si geme, si muore.
> Difenditi, o core!

Second unit
repeated:

> Speranza tradita
> a colpo di pene
> tra lacci e catene
> all'armi l'invita.
> Intrepida ardita
> ne rischi di morte
> non cura la sorte,
> minaccie e rigore.

Closing verse:

> Difenditi, amore!

Second unit
repeated again:

> Sensa aura di scampo
> gelosi desiri
> a suon de sospiri
> ti chiamano in campo.
> La fiamma d'un lampo
> ancor che sia solo
> può toglierti il volo,
> rapirti l'honore.

Closing verse:

> Difenditi, amore!

If Luigi had wished, he could have formed a strophic ternary cantata by taking the opening quatrain and one of the additional texts of the second unit of the rounded binary cantata and setting them to the music of the ternary first and second units. Or he could have composed a rondo by following the second statement of the ternary first unit with a repetition of its second unit set to one of the two additional texts given in the rounded binary version and concluding with the recapitulation of the refrain *Difenditi, o core*.

As the texts quoted above demonstrate, the refrain verses—those at the close of the strophic binary and rounded binary second units, as well as the first units of the ternary and rondo cantatas—are usually exhortative, imperative, admonitory, pleading: exclamatory verses that share an elemental affective quality that creates considerable impact. These verses, in fact, often embody the main point of the text. Thus even in those cantatas whose refrain verses are declarative, the reprise has the evident purpose of reasserting the thought developed in the rest of the text.

Another trait of the strophic texts is a pronounced syntactical parallelism in the construction of the stanzas. In the rondo and rounded binary whose second units are repeated strophically, this parallelism consists in the recurrence of questions, declarative statements and exclamations in corresponding places of the strophes. In the ternary, rounded binary and binary cantatas that are repeated in their entirety with new text, the parallelism is usually more extensive, entailing as well the recurrence of particular words in corresponding places, or of a particular order of verb, noun and adjective. The first units of the binary *Ch'io sospiri* and *Mio cor, di che paventi*, the ternary *Fanciulle, tenete* and *Perche chieder* (see pp. 42-44), the rounded binary *Rendetevi, pensieri* and *Su, su, begl'occhi*, for example, are related in this manner:

1st strophe:	Ch'io sospiri al vostro foco, ch'io languisca, impallidisca, occhi belli, occhi cari, ahi, vi par poco!
2nd strophe:	Ch'io non ami vostri rai, non adori vostri ardori, occhi belli, occhi cari, ahi, non fia mai!
3rd strophe:	Ch'io già mai chieggia pietate del mio mal ben che mortale, occhi belli, occhi cari, ahi, v'ingannate!
1st strophe:	Mio cor, di che paventi? Soffri costante pene, affanni, tormenti!
2nd strophe:	Mio cor, perche respiri? Soffri costante doglie, inganni, martiri!
3rd strophe:	Mio cor, non stare in pene. Soffri costante strali, incendiy, catene!
1st strophe:	Fanciulle, tenete il guardo a voi!
2nd strophe:	Fanciulle, tenete all'erta il core!
1st strophe:	Rendetevi, pensieri, non contrastate più!
2nd strophe:	Fermatevi, desiri, deh, chiedete merce!
1st strophe:	Su, su, begl'occhi, su, su! Date pace al mio core che langue d'amore; nol ferite, tradite già più!
2nd strophe:	Su, su, bei labri, su su! Deh, temprate il veleno che chiude nel seno; nol crescete, nudrite già più!

Similarly, the second units of the binary *Un tiranno* and *Ragion mi dice*, and the ternary and rounded binary cantatas quoted above (for the strophes of *Perche chieder*, see pp. 42-44 below):

1st strophe:	Hor tra gelidi timori teme e trema il petto mio. Hor tra fervidi dolori fiamma e cenere son io.

Così tra varie tempre
son dannato a gelare et arder sempre.

2nd strophe: Hor tra gelide amarezze
apro, ohime, cent'occhi e cento.
Hor tra fervide dolcezze
d'ogni lume il guardo ho spento.
Così m'ha fatto amore
un argo cieco et un gelato ardore.

—Un tiranno

1st strophe: Pupille care,
vi lascierò.
No, no,
raddoppiate l'ardore!
Tace, ragion, dove consiglia amore!

2nd strophe: Pupille amate,
vi fuggirò.
No, no,
saettate rigore!
Tace, ragion, dove consiglia amore!

—Ragion mi dice

1st strophe: Eccolo che sen viene,
tutto fe, tutto spene,
a farvi guerra.

2nd strophe: Eccolo che sen riede,
tutto amor, tutto fede,
a farvi guerra.

—Fanciulle

1st strophe: Chi sa, forse, chi sa?
Vincitrice beltà
fia che vibri nel sen strali men fieri.
Rendetevi, pensieri!

2nd strophe: Chi sa, forse, chi sa?
L'empia che fe non ha
fia che forse pietosa un dì si giri.
Fermatevi, desiri!

—Rendetevi

1st strophe: Vostri crude e fieri sguardi
sono dardi onde a morte ogn'hor si va.

2nd strophe: Vostri sdegni e rei furori
                    son dolori per cui l'alma a morte va.

        —Su, su

Correspondences of this kind prevail especially in the concluding verses of the binary strophes:

1st strophe: In quel labbro ogni riso, ahi, ch'è saetta!

2nd strophe: In quel labbro ogn'accento, ahi, ch'è mortale!

        —Due labbra di rose

1st strophe: E breve campo a due guerrieri un seno.

2nd strophe: E picciol regno a due tiranni un core.

        —Due feroci guerrieri

1st strophe: Perch'è l'istessa cosa affatto, affatto,
                    il languir per amor e l'esser matto!

2nd strophe: Perch'è tutto uno a far il pazzarello,
                    l'esser amante è perder il cervello!

3rd strophe: Perche non si puo dir che simpatia
                    hanno insieme l'amore e la pazzia!

        —Chi d'amor sin ai capelli

1st strophe: Ma hor ch'io so come saetti et ardi,
                    ch'io m'innamor più, Dio mene guardi!

2nd strophe: Ma hor ch'io so come aggiacciando avvampi,
                    ch'io m'innamor più, Dio meme scampi!

        —All'hor

1st strophe: Parla, parla, mio core, parla codardo,
                    avvivar può mill'alme un reggio sguardo!

2nd strophe: Parla, parla, mio core, parla insensato,
                    cede ai reggi la sorte e serve il fato!

3rd strophe: Parla, parla, mio core, lascia il timore,
                    finche parla la lingua e viva il core!

        —O cieli, pietà

In *Occhi soavi*, where the order of words is maintained in parallel qualifying verses, the structural correspondence coincides with the naming of entirely diverse qualities:

1st strophe: Vi dirò rubelle, vi dirò perverse!

2nd strophe: Vi dirò beate, vi dirò divine!

The principle of strophic parallelism is that one strophe continues the meaning of the other and is structured like the other. Parallelism makes it possible to retain one musical setting for the various strophes. Thus a musical passage that responds to a particular *affetto* is appropriately retained for the various strophes when the same *affetto* is evoked in each at the same place. For example, in the first unit of the binary cantata *Horche di marte*, at the fourth verse "alla guerra, all guerra, all'armi, all'armi!" there is a change from 4/4 to an energetic movement in 3/4. The 3/4 passages fits the second strophe equally well, for the fourth verse there is "sfidi pur alla guerra, all'armi, all'armi!"

Still another characteristic of all four cantata types is that texts entirely of verses of an odd number of syllables (impari verses), primarily heptasyllables and hendecasyllables, or verses of an even number of syllables (pari verses), primarily hexasyllables and octosyllables, are more prevalent than texts of mixed verses.[11] I have investigated this aspect of the cantata texts primarily in order to determine whether there is a correlation between the poetic and musical meters. For example, one finds that metric stability in an arietta corta is conjoined more than 75 percent of the time with a text of unmixed verses. This matter of the correlation of meter and text is discussed below, pp. 51-52.

In respect to poetic meter, it is remarkable that the rounded binary, ternary and rondo texts again show a strong relationship and differ from the binary texts in that half of them are entirely or almost entirely of pari verses, whereas the binary texts are for the most part entirely of impari verses.[12] The rounded binary, ternary and rondo texts differ from the binary texts in still another way. Few of them conclude with a hendecasyllable, whereas the closing hendecasyllable is a trait of the binary texts— 83 end with a line of this length. This trait has a corresponding musical one—the final verse is repeated several times and given an extended setting. In fact, in many cantatas it makes up most of the second unit. This is not at all characteristic of the ternary and rondo cantatas. In the rounded binary cantatas the final verse of the second unit is also emphasized musically, but its setting is usually not as extended as in the simple binary.

The texts quoted below represent common poetic structures. The first is an example of a binary text of one strophe formed of two units of different lengths, entirely of impari verses and closing with a hendecasyllable and a rhyming couplet. The second, an example in which strophic parallelism is very much in evidence, is a binary text of three strophes with a recurring final verse, a refrain. Another characteristic is the striking contrast between the successive segments of each strophe: the narrative quatrain that is the first unit, the meditation that forms the first half of the second unit, and the plea that concludes the cantata beginning with a vocative and concluding with an exhortative exclamation. The third example is a ternary text of three strophes that is typical in all respects except one: the rhyming couplet that concludes the second unit is typical of binary second units, but exceptional in ternary texts. Characteristically the first unit is a quatrain, the second unit is about twice as long as the first, and the verses are all pari. The fourth text, a rondo, is similar to the previous one—the first unit is a quatrain, the second unit is twice as long as the first and the verses are all pari. In this example we find the most typical rhyme scheme of the second unit: cddcceea; and the prevailing trait of ternary and rondo texts: the last verse of each of the various stanzas of the second unit rhymes with the first verse of the first unit. The rounded binary texts are well exemplified in *Ohime, madre* and *Difenditi, amore*, quoted above, pp. 34 and 35, respectively. Both texts have the abbreviated strophic form characteristic of their group alone. In both the verses are pari; the first is of octosyllables, the second is of hexasyllables. The first unit has the usual envelope design, the penultimate verse of each stanza of the second unit rhymes with the first verse of the first unit (which also forms the close of each of these stanzas), and the overall rhyme scheme is the typical AbbaA cddcceeA. Both examples, with the designated alterations in the recapitulation schemes, could be ternary and rondo texts.

1.   Ahi, quante volte io moro!
     E morendo vi chieggio
     amorosa pietade,
     occhi ch'adoro.

     E voi, lieve ristoro
     mai sempre al cor negate.
     Ma per tanta beltade
     nel grave ardor ch'io sento
     m'è riposo il penar, pace il tormento!

                    I

2.   Quando spiega la notte humida l'ali

al mondo nuntia di giocondo oblio,
depongono i mortali
ogni pensier più rio.

Et io traffitt'il seno
per ombre oscure e chete
oh ritrovassi almeno
all'amaro veghiar dolce quiete!
Sonno, soave speme
de più noiosi affanni,
stendi sovra di me tacito i vanni.
Soccorri alle mie pene!

II

Quando sul carro d'immortale argento
Cintia trascorre i luminosi giri,
io muovo il pie non lento
nuovi a cercar martiri.

E la m'aggiro e torno
ove splende quel sole
ch'all'altro sol fa scorno
sol che solo il mio cor sospira e vuole.
Sonno, diletta speme
di chi piangendo langue,
non è più pianto quel ch'io verso, è sangue.
Soccorri alle mie pene!

III

Quando del biondo crin gl'aurei tesori
riporta Febo a non veduto polo,
dormon sul parto i fiori,
ferman gl'augelli il volo.

Io tra duri lamenti
non chiudo al sonno i lumi
che d'allegrezza spenti
troppo fiero martir converte in fiumi.
Sonno, soave spene
d'un tormentato core,
s'amor non fia pietà del mio dolore,
soccorri alle mie pene!

I

3.   Perche chieder com'io sto
mentr'il puoi saper da te?
Da che sono fuor di me

di me nuova più non ho.

Io non so
che si faccia e come stia
da che s'è partita
l'alma mia.
Se n'andrò per la ferita
che faceste nel mio seno,
e passò in un baleno
nel tuo core a miglior vita.
E se in esso non è più
sai tu sole che ne fu.

Perche chieder com'io sto
mentr'il puoi saper da te?
Da che sono fuor di me
di me nuova più non ho.

II

Perche cerchi come sta
chi sta ben se l'ami tu?
Chi sol quanto l'ami più
tanto meglio se la fa.

Non si sa
che si faccia e come stia
da che alberga in altrui petto
l'alma mia.

Sene venne per diletto
a far vita nel tuo cuore,
e 'l tuo dolce e caro amore
gli donò miglior ricetto.
E se in esso più non è
ne dimando il conto a te.

Perche cerchi come sta
chi sta ben se l'ami tu?
Chi sol quanto l'ami più,
tanto meglio se la fa.

III

A che chieder il perche
mesta o lieta mene vo?
Tal'io son qual farmi può
il tuo amore e la tua fe.

Chiedo a te
che si faccia e come stia
da che sta come tu vuoi
l'alma mia.
Non son più gl'arbitry suoi
quei che dan le gioie e pene
ma in dolcissime catene
serve solo a cenni tuoi.
E qual vita goderà
se nol dici, non si sa.

A che chieder il perche
mesta o lieta meno vo?
Tal'io son qual farmi può
il tuo amore e la tua fe.

4.   La bella che mi contenta
ha volto che spira amore,
ma vaga del suo rigore,
non gode se non tormenta.

Chi teme il volo d'un strale
non speri trovar pietà,
col vezzo de la beltà
fierezza va sempre equale.
Ferita quando è mortale,
discopre del cor la fe,
e muta chiede merce
dal guardo che fiamme avventa.

La bella che mi contenta
ha volto che spira amore,
ma vaga del suo rigore,
non gode se non tormenta.

Un alma che brama vita
adora chi la tradì,
s'amore pria la ferì,
risorge più sempre ardita.
Mia fede cosi tradita
sue tempie mai non cangiò,
ch'io sprezzi chi m'impiagò
amore non lo consenta.

La bella che mi contenta
ha volto che spira amore,
ma vaga del suo rigore,
non gode se non tormenta.

The texts of the few rondo cantatas of three or more units, unlike those of the strophic rondos, do not usually have symmetrical stanzas between statements of the refrain.[13] The second and third units have texts that differ in number of lines, in rhyme scheme and in verse lengths:

> Su la veglia d'una speme
> il mio cor penando sta.
> Deh, porgete al suo mal qualche pietà!

> Stratiato dal dolore
> non sentitc come geme?
> E tiranno ben quel core
> che ristoro non gli da.

> Su la veglia d'una speme
> il mio cor penando sta.
> Deh, porgete al suo mal qualche pietà!

> O voi che mirate
> l'atroce martire
> ch'infida beltate
> m'astringe a soffrire,
> su, deh, pietosi, porgetemi aita!
> Che quasi di vita
> è priva quest'anima.
> Il duol m'esanima,
> languisco, mi moro
> ne trovo ristoro
> alle mie doglie estreme.

> Su la veglia d'una speme
> il mio cor penando sta.
> Deh, porgete al suo mal qualche pietà!

Text Repetition. In the cantatas of all four groups, text repetition almost invariably occurs at the close of the unit that terminates the cantata—the second unit of the binary and rounded binary, the first of the ternary and rondo cantatas. But, as I mentioned before, there is usually more repetition at the close of the binary cantata than anywhere else. Text repetition is also common at the close of the first unit of the binary and rounded binary cantatas and occurs occasionally at the close of the second unit of the ternary and rondo cantatas, although it is not common. In some cantatas there is text repetition in the opening phrases, but this is not a general trait except in the binary ensembles, most of which have short texts; here verse repetition prevails throughout the cantata. As one would expect, sequence and musical repetition usually occur where there is text repetition. This is discussed below, p. 66.

Rarely is a whole stanza or an entire group of verses repeated as a whole. In the binary cantatas, *Amor*, *con dolci* and *Io ero* and the rondo *E si credi*, where this happens, the second statement of the whole first-unit quatrain is given a new musical setting; the procedure is employed in place of repetition of the closing words. An unusual manner of setting this kind of repetition is found in the aria di più parti *Ardo*, *sospiro*. Here the second statement of the first unit of text, which is repeated as in the ariette mentioned above, is given the original setting transposed at the fourth below. This is the only example I know in the cantata repertory of a complete musical unit repeated in the key of the dominant.

Another unique example of text repetition of a whole group of verses occurs in the second unit of the rondo *Speranze, che dite* (ex. XXVII). Here all the verses of the second unit excepting the final reprise verse from the close of the unit are repeated, using the original setting at pitch, fully written out. It is very likely that the repetition is made in order to balance this unit of seven verses against the longer third unit and its strophic repetition, each of 11 verses. Because of the repetition the lengths of these units are approximately the same: second unit: 3/4, 36 measures; third and fourth units: 3/4, 38 measures. A close look at the text of this cantata reveals that in its original form the text was probably meant to be a strophic binary cantata with concluding refrain. It consisted of three symmetrical strophes, each of ten verses, the last verse recurring as refrain. From the first strophe of this text a refrain was formed—the third and fourth verses[14]—and a second rondo unit consisting of the remaining five verses and the concluding reprise, which includes the second verse. The second and third strophes became the second and third rondo strophes:

Strophic binary text	Rondo text	
I		Refrain:
Speranze, che dite,	Speranze, che dite,	
ancora credete?	ancora credete?	
Andate che siete	Andate che siete	
speranze fallite!	speranze fallite!	
		2nd unit:
Ho fatto col pianto	Ho fatto col pianto	
già l'ultime prove,	già l'ultime prove,	
ne punto si move	ne punto si move	
dal empio suo vanto.	dal empio suo vanto.	
Chi vuol che languite?	Chi vuol che languite?	
Speranze, che dite?		repeated:

Ho fatto col pianto
già l'ultime prove,
ne punto si move
dal empio suo vanto.
Chi vuol che languite?

conclusion:

Speranze, che dite,
ancora credete?

Refrain:

Andate che siete
speranze fallite!

3rd unit:

II

Nel freddo suo centro
quel perfido core
è pien di rigore,
o ch'altro v'è dentro

Tropp'oltre il costume
resist'a i sospiri
e tien per deliri
ch'amore sia nume,
che faccia ferite.
Speranze, che dite?

Nel freddo suo centro
quel perfido core
è pien di rigore,
o ch'altro v'è dentro.

Tropp'oltre il costume
resist'a i sospiri
e tien per deliri
ch'amore sia nume,
che faccia ferite.

conclusion:

Speranze, che dite,
ancora credete?

refrain:

Andate che siete
speranze fallite!

III

Si frange una pietra
all'onda cadente,
ma un tono sovente
all'onda s'impetra.

Di fede costanza
le glorie più altiere
son belle chimere
senz'altra sostanza
che pene infinite.
Speranze, che dite?

4th unit:

Si frange una pietra
all'ondo cadente,
ma un tono sovente
all'onda s'impetra.

Di fede costanza
le glorie più altiere
son belle chimere
senz'altra sostanza
che pene infinite.

conclusion:

Speranze, che dite,
ancora credete?

                                    refrain:

Andate che siete
speranze fallite!

Notation. With very few exceptions the two units are clearly separated by double bars at the close of the first unit.[15] Repeat dots are usually found at this place in the simple binary cantatas, but not in the rounded binary cantatas. In the ternary and rondo cantatas repeat dots do not normally occur anywhere. The rondo and ternary first units usually conclude with double bars and/or a wavy line, sometimes drawn with elaborate flourishes, that signifies "fine" and is occasionally followed by this reminder. The binary second units close in the same way as the rondo and ternary first units: a breve with a fermata, double bar and/or wavy line, and very rarely repeat dots.[16] This is due, of course, to the fact that these units conclude their respective cantata types.

Because the rondo and ternary second units lead directly into the reprise of the first unit, rarely is there any sign of demarcation at their close. Usually the first notes or the first measures of the first unit are notated with or, less often, without one of the rubrics: *da capo*, *ut supra* or *dal segno*. Occasionally the recapitulation is written out—this usually happens only when there is some variation or change in the music, but sometimes there is no reason other than the copyist's habit of making a complete and careful copy. In fact, except in elegantly notated manuscripts like *I* Rvat, 4200, 4208, 4150; Rc, 2477; G1, A.5.Cass; Fc, D 2357; Bc *Q* 50; and *F* Pthibault, G.T.3, probably copied by professionals for wealthy noblemen or to be given as a gift, strophic repetitions are usually not written out; only the new text of the units to be repeated strophically is notated—text for both units of the binary and ternary cantatas, and text for the second unit of the rondos and of the rounded binary cantatas having the form a/ b/ b/. The text for strophic repetition is usually notated at the close of the cantata, often on a separate page. In a few rondos, however, the text for the repetition of the second unit is given below its bass line.[17] When this is done, the copyist either writes a rubric for the recapitulation of the refrain after each of the stanzas of the second unit, or he simply writes one after the first stanza, or he writes out the refrain with no rubric at all. In the case of either of the last mentioned procedures, the cantata seems to have the form A b b A, since the return of the refrain between the second unit and its repetition is not specified.[18] But this is not intended. Concordances prove that the form is the usual rondo A b A b A.

In quite a number of manuscripts the designations "la," "Pa," or "Prima" and "2a" appear. These designations, which mean "prima strofa" and "seconda strofa," usually occur in the rondos, seldom in the other cantatas. In the rondos "Pa" is placed at the beginning of the second unit, "2a," at the beginning of the strophic repetition of the second unit, or its second stanza. In the few cases where "2a" appears in the binary cantatas, it precedes the text for the strophic repetition of both units. In the rounded binary cantatas, however, it is used as in the rondos—"2a" signifies the second set of verses for the second unit. Usually the rondo first unit is unmarked, but in a few manuscripts the terms "Streviglio" and "Intercalare," both meaning "refrain," refer to it. "Streviglio" was proably a common term, for in Cesti's famous parody cantata, *Aspettate*, it is used in a reference to the rondo as a favorite form of composition: ". . . se qual ch'uno gli lavora l'estriviglio e un par di stanze."[19]

One finds in comparing the notational practices in different manuscripts, and also in comparing the manner of notating a single cantata in various concordances, that discrepancies in the notation both of a cantata type and of an individual piece are quite common. Many manuscripts are the work of several copyists who did not all observe the same conventions. There are also manuscripts copied by a single hand that show many inconsistencies. But there are sources where certain conventions of notation are regularly used. These are notated by professional copyists and musicians (see, for example, *I* Rvat, 4208; *F* Pbn, Rés Vm 7 59 and 102, Vm 7 6). The several notational traits that I have described above are those observed in these sources.

Problems of notation that deserve investigation, but are beyond the scope of this work, are the realization of the basso continuo, usually notated with few or no figures and accidentals; the interpretation of black notation in passages where it is not limited to hemiola, and the probable tempo implications of the various metric signatures. Another problem requiring investigation concerns the transcription of the freely shifting meter, which is not generally indicated in the sources by the exact placing of barlines or the insertion of metric signatures. The concordances, in fact, usually disagree in the placing of the barlines. In the examples quoted in the text and in the Appendix, the barlines are placed as they appear in one of the sources; they have not been readjusted. The problem of accidentals is treated in the introduction to Volume 2.

Dimensions. Although no two cantatas are exactly the same size, most occupy between 40 and 60 notated measures and last in time between one-and-one-half and two minutes. These statistics refer to the two successive units of the ariette corte without strophic repetitions and recapitulations. The ternary and rondo two unit sections tend to be closer to one-and-one-half minutes whereas the binary and rounded binary two unit sections tend to be closer to two minutes in length. In all but the rounded binary group and irrespective of the dimensions of the whole, the second unit is generally slightly longer than the first. In the ternary and rondo cantatas this is mostly due to the greater length of the text of the second unit; but in the binary cantatas, the respective lengths of the two units are not determined by the number of verses set in each. As was mentioned earlier, there is much repetition of the concluding verse of the binary text that extends the second unit in length; there is also some repetition of text in the first unit that is not characteristic of the beginning of the second unit. For example, the first unit of *Si o no*, a quatrain, occupies 21½ measures of 6/2; the tercet that follows and introduces the final segment is set to five measures of recitative. The concluding couplet occupies 27 measures of 6/4 and a final phrase, more slowly paced, of five measures of duple meter. The equality of the two units, or the slightly greater length of the first unit in 11 of the 19 rounded binary cantatas, derives in large part from the recurrence and repetition of the first verse in the closing segment of the first unit, from the repetition of the same verse in the introductory segment, and from the fact that the closure of the second unit, quoted from the first unit, is generally not as long as in the simple binary.

Normally the shortest segment in any of the cantatas is that where there is little or no text repetition. In all four groups, this tends to be the first part of the second unit; occasional melismatic lengthenings do not alter the overall picture. That there is a close relationship between musical length and text repetition is confirmed by the fact that the longest cantatas, mostly ensembles, are those where text repetition is prevalent from beginning to end. One cannot always judge the dimensions of a cantata by its number of measures. Since about half the cantatas are composed with change of meter, one must take into account the different tempi and the varying number of beats in the different measures. In the ternary cantatas *Perche chieder* and *Querelatevi*, for example, the number of measures in the second unit is smaller than in the first, but the change from triple to slower-paced duple including phrases of recitative gives the second unit length and weight. A passage of aria in common-time takes longer to perform than a passage of the same number of measures of 6/4 or 6/8 meter. Similarly a passage of arioso-recitative in common time requires more time than a passage of the same number of measures of 6/2.

Taking these factors into account, the following can be cited as examples of the typical layout of each of the four types of the ariette corte: the binary *Se nell'arsura* (ex. I), *Quando spiega* (ex. II, any one of the three strophes), *Ho perduto*, *Addio*, *perfida*; the rounded binary *Difenditi, amore* (ex. III), *Disperati, ch'aspetti* (ex. IV), *Respira core* (ex. V), *Uscite di porto* (ex. VI); the ternary *Difenditi, o core* (ex. VII), *E d'amore*, *Fanciulle tenete*, *Un cor*; the rondos *Che cosa* (ex. VIII), *Hor guardate* (ex. IX), *Mi contento*, *Quanto è credulo*. The shortest cantatas in the four groups are the binary *Come tosto* and *Precorrea* (ex. X, any one of the four strophes), the rounded binary *Non mi fate* (ex. XI), the ternary *Amor, e perche* (ex. XII), and the rondos *A chi, lasso* and *Chi non sa fingere* (this last mentioned, lasting less than a minute even at moderate tempo, is probably the shortest of all the ariette). Among the longest are the binary duos *Amor con dolci*, *Occhi belli, occhi miei*, *Occhi quei vaghi*; the rounded binary duo *Risolvetevi* (ex. XIII), and the rondo duo *Speranze, sentite* (ex. XIV).

Metric-Organization. Triple meter prevails in all four groups—85 of the 216 ariette are composed entirely in 6/4 or 3/4, or somewhat less often, in 6/2 or 3/2;[20] 6/8 is the least common of the triple meters.[21] The 25 cantatas entirely in duple meter[22] are not consistently composed in aria style from beginning to end; in many of them recitative and arioso form one unit or part of a unit, and in several one finds concitato passages.

One hundred and six cantatas, almost half of the total, are composed with one or more metric changes. The majority of these are binary cantatas—only one third of the rounded binary, ternary and rondo cantatas display metric change compared to more than half of the binary. The greater number of metric changes in the binary group corresponds to a strong tendency towards segmentation of the second unit in this type, a trait not characteristic of the other groups. This segmentation often goes hand in hand with changes of meter.

Whereas there is a high degree of correlation between metric and poetic schemes in the group of cantatas where no metric changes occur—80 of the 110 have texts all of one kind of verse or all of unmixed pari or impari[23]—this same degree of correlation is not present in the cantatas where metric change occurs. By and large, metric change is independent of the text and is determined by formal conventions—in all four groups, the contrast of the two units, and in the binary, the use of recitative as an introductory or transitional passage within the second unit to set off the concluding segment.[24] Other conventions, less prevalent than the two mentioned above, include the setting off of the introductory passage of the first unit,[25] the return to the meter of this passage at the close of the first units having the envelope design, and the use of duple meter at the close of a unit in triple meter to retard the movement or to allow for an unmeasured, rhapsodic melisma.[26]

A significant minority of the prevalent conventional changes—those articulating the formal design—also correspond with changes in the poetic structure, especially in rounded binary, ternary and rondo cantatas.[27] In the cantatas of these three groups, where metric change occurs with texts of mixed verses, contrast between groups of verses of different lengths often coincides with metric contrast. The highest degree of correlation between poetic and musical meters occurs in the rounded binary cantatas. Here one finds that all but one of the cantatas of unmixed verses are in one meter from beginning to end, and that all the cantatas of mixed verses are set with changes of meter that correspond with the poetic structure. In the miniature cantata *Non mi fate mentire* (ex. XI), the one rounded binary cantata where metric change does not coincide with varying verse lengths, the change responds to another aspect of the text. It directs attention to the text content emphasizing the difference between the recurring exclamation, the reprise verse "Non mi fate mentire!," and the declarative statement it enframes. The exclamation is set each time in 6/4 meter; the two other passages—each is only the length of a phrase—are both recitatives.

Possibly the reason for the higher degree of correlation in this group of cantatas than in the similarly constructed rondo and ternary groups, is that the singular trait of the rounded binary group is correspondence between the two units, whereas the rondo and ternary units tend to be differentiated. Hence in these two groups there are texts of unmixed verses composed with conventional metric changes.[28]

The binary cantatas show the least correlation between metric and poetic designs. The texts of the binary cantatas, one should recall, are quite different from those of the other three groups. Metric contrast appears to be primarily a means of articulating a conventional formal design. As I have already mentioned, metric change most often sets off the concluding segment of the second unit, which is usually composed in triple meter,[29] and is frequently preceded by a passage in recitative. This segment is generally the setting of a gnomic verse or of a morale—the final verse or couplet which serves, in 42 of the strophic pieces, as a recurring refrain. Thus segmentation also serves as a means of underscoring the text content.

In the binary cantatas, as in the other groups, there appears to be a general convention requiring that the first unit remain in one meter. When metric change occurs, it is usually to set off the introductory passage or to reflect a particularly striking shift in the poetry. Perhaps the reason for the rarity of metric change in this unit is the relative brevity of the text in all four groups, and the homogeneous quality of the verses.

Where metric change can be accounted for neither by apparent conventions of the formal design nor by a particular versification scheme, its motivation is generally to be found in the imagery, syntax, mood, or general content of the accompanying text. Occasionally such change is a means of emphasizing a particular word or verse, or creates or underscores the contrast between two clauses—a narrative and a meditative clause, a declarative and an exclamatory or interrogative one, or a conditional and an assertive one.[30] Such shifts of mood are usually present in those cantatas with an unusual amount of metric fluctuation. For example, in *Che cosa mi dite* (ex. VIII), two changes of meter occur in the refrain, another change from the refrain to the strophe, and three changes within the strophe. The changes are never erratic, but fit the poetic structure, the content of the text and the particular function of the passage. The first change sets off the introductory segment; the choice of 6/8 for the motto opening was no doubt influenced by the fact that the verse "Che cosa mi dite?" is a hexasyllable. The change to 3/4 at the beginning of the next phrase coincides not only with a shift in verse length (from a hexasyllable to an octosyllabe and two quadrisyllables), but also with a reference to "change" that is literally realized by the setting:

> Che si cangino in contenti
> i tormenti
> che soffrite?

In the conclusion, a Phrygian cadence appropriate for the intense expression of the second question, the opening verse returns and with it the 6/8 meter. Although the harmony is static, the vigorous quality of the 6/8 movement lends this brief phrase a sense of excitement and urgency. An altogether different interpretation of the verse follows in the lyrical concluding passage that is composed in the slower 3/4 meter of the inner phrase. With the shift to narration in hendecasyllables at the beginning of the second unit, the style and meter change; a passage in recitative initiates the second unit. But when the narration gives way to the strong declarative statement "nel'alma si pente/ de vari pensieri!" there is a return to 6/8 (signed 3/8 at this point in the example). Here again 6/8 is correlated to hexasyllables. Immediately following this declaration, the shift to a pair of hendecasyllabic exhortative verses coincides with a change to arioso-recitative. For the final verses of the second unit, three hexasyllables, Luigi returns once more to 6/8, presumably in preparation for the return of the opening line.

As I have indicated, there is an apparent correlation between the use of 6/8 meter and the presence in the poetry of one or more hexasyllables, usually exhortative in nature. This is true not only of cantatas like *Che cosa mi dite*, where there is a shift of mood and a contrast between verse lengths, but also of entire movements in 6/8.[31]

There is a similar, though less pronounced, correlation between aria-style passages in duple meter and the presence in the text of octosyllables. This does not appear to be associated with any particular kind of mood. Although only eight of the 37 texts consisting entirely of octosyllables are set in duple meter throughout, no other verse length appears as consistently with passages of aria in common-time as does this one.[32] Another feature of the particular aria style often associated with octosyllables is a migrating motive that appears in about 20 cantatas. This recurring motive is discussed below, p. 77.

As was mentioned at the beginning of this discussion regarding metric organization, cantatas entirely in duple meter are not consistently composed in one style; changes in style in these cantatas are often textually motivated, corresponding to shifts of mood in the poetry. For example, the narrative and descriptive opening verses of *Quando spiega* (ex. II; see above, pp. 41-42 for text) which, in the succession of strophes, speak of activities of nature at various times during the 24-hour cycle, are set in recitative. The immobile, austere beginning establishes both the mood and the tonality. The recitative concludes with a melismatic passage that is apparently purely structural in function, serving to articulate the close of the first unit; but in the third strophe it is composed with the descriptive noun "volo" that often inspires increased melodic activity. In fact, in this strophe the melisma is more extended than in either of the previous strophes. The melisma leads with theatrical emphasis to the cadence—the melody falls an octave from its climactic tone to the final notes of the phrase. (In the second strophe the fall is even more dramatic—an eleventh.) Such a gesture is usually found only in cadences concluding a unit. The inner feelings of the protagonist, the utterance of torment that forms the first part of the second unit, are composed in more passionate recitative. Here the affective quality of the melodic line is enhanced by the descending skips of a minor seventh and a diminished fifth. This segment moves away from the primary tonality (E-flat) modulating to the relative minor and concludes with an eloquent Phrygian cadence in that key. With a return to the major tonic, an entirely new movement begins with the lyric call to sleep "Sonno, soave speme di più noiosi affanni!" the beginning of the final quatrain of the text. Its setting is a phrase of aria. This merges with the next phrase, again recitative and returning to the affective mood of the relative minor. The change in style underscores the change from the exclamatory vocative to the protagonist's plea "stendi sovra di me tacito i vanni." For the repeated exhortative exclamation with which the cantata concludes, Luigi composes a new aria passage setting this verse, the refrain, apart from the preceding segment of the second unit. Like the previous passage in aria, this one returns to the original major tonality. Thus in a cantata whose text of impari verses is composed with no change of meter, we find contrasting passages of recitative and aria chosen not arbitrarily, but with sensitive response to the various moods of the poem.

In other cases this response may be conspicuously lacking—occasionally to such a degree that the setting seems not to follow the text at all. For example, there are texts whose groups of contrasting verse lengths suggest the conventional metric division of the two units, yet whose music is composed either with no metric change at all, or with a metric change that does not correspond to the poetry.[33] Evidently the shape of these cantatas is determined primarily by factors other than textual. I have been unable to discover any consistent pattern of relationships that might explain these widely divergent degrees of responsiveness to poetic structure and content. It is a subject deserving of further study.

The following chart will serve to recall some of the facts discussed above:

	Binary	R. Binary	Ternary	Rondo	All
Cantatas entirely in triple meter with no metric change:	39	13	9	24	85
Entirely in duple meter:	16	1	3	5	25
Total cantatas without metric change:	55	14	12	29	110
Texts entirely or almost entirely of one kind of verse set with metric change:	42	0	6	11	60
The same set without metric change:	36	14	7	23	80
Texts of mixed verses set with metric change:	24	5	4	14	46
The same set without metric change:	19	0	5	6	30
Cantatas with one or more metric changes:	66	5	10	25	106

Tonal Characteristics. Though the complex issues of seventeenth-century tonality lie largely beyond the scope of this discussion, it can be unequivocally asserted that a single tonal center underlies each of Luigi's cantatas, acting as a prime determinant of both local contexts and of overall structure. In approximately three quarters of the cantatas, the mode erected around this center is a minor one. The most common tonalities, in order of their relative frequency, are C, E, D, A and G minor. A few pieces are in F minor (nine) and one (*O dura*) is in B-flat minor. Proportionately more ensembles are composed in the major tonalities than are solo pieces. In fact, nearly half of the ensembles are in the major mode. The major tonalities most frequently used are B-flat, C, D and F. There are only five cantatas in E major, five in A, three in E-flat. A striking peculiarity is the frequent occurrence of the major mode with triple meter and with hexasyllable verses; the key of B-flat is the favorite key for the setting of hexasyllables.[34]

All but 14 of the first units of the ariette corte conclude with a perfect cadence in the tonality announced in the introductory phrase—the home key. Among the exceptions is the single strict ostinato cantata, the rondo *La bella più bella*; both its units conclude with an imperfect cadence to the tonic. Of the 13 other exceptions, two close with a perfect cadence in the key of the minor dominant,[35] and 11 close with a Phrygian cadence on the dominant.[36] In three of the latter, the choice of cadence seems to relate to the text content.[37] The Phrygian close is a concomitant of the doubt and despair evoked in the texts—each of the three concludes with a rhetorical question whose emotional quality is appropriately underscored by the Phrygian cadence. That the choice of cadence was most certainly influenced by the text is evident in the rondo *Che dici* where at the close of the cantata the positive declaration "L'ha detto il mio core!" replaces the refrain verse "Che dici, mio core?" With the change of text goes a corresponding change in the musical setting; the declaration concludes with a perfect cadence to the tonic.

The concluding segment of the second units of the binary and rounded binary cantatas almost invariably confirms the tonality announced and established in the first unit.[38] Due to their different function in the formal designs, the second units of the ternary and rondo groups, contained as they are within statements of the first unit-refrain, do not need to reaffirm the primary tonality. Despite this, more than half of them do close in the home key, with either a perfect or an imperfect cadence or, occasionally, with a semi-cadence to the dominant. This fact is significant in that it points to the predominant emphasis on the central tonality that is characteristic of both units in all four groups. Those second units that do not conclude in the tonic close in keys closely related to it: the minor dominant, the relative minor, the subdominant, and the relative major, in order of frequency. These statistics account for all but two of the ternary and rondo second units: a ternary that ends with a cadence in the key of the minor supertonic, and a rondo that closes in the key of the minor mediant.

Beyond those anchoring points where the tonality is announced and reaffirmed, the cadence disposition is flexible. Modulations occur in both units; their choice, duration, number and sequence vary considerably from cantata to cantata. Phrases cadencing in the tonic key area, Phrygian cadences on the dominant as well as perfect and imperfect cadences on the tonic intermingle with phrases cadencing in the secondary degrees. However, in many binary and rounded binary cantatas one finds that the secondary degrees predominate at the close of the inner phrases, especially in the second unit. The primary tonality is not jeopardized by these passing modulations—each usually lasts no more than one or two phrases. Moreover, the return of the tonic in the concluding segment is more effective because of its absence in the preceding passages.

The brief modulations are excursions from the tonic to one or another of its related degrees. Usually no more than four, and no fewer than three key areas other than that of the tonic are touched upon in the course of the two units.[39] The most common modulations in cantatas in the minor mode are, in their order of frequency, to the relative major, the minor dominant, the seventh degree (the relative major of the dominant), and the minor subdominant.[40] Modulations to the major subdominant, the major submediant, the supertonic and the minor seventh degree (the minor subdominant of the subdominant) occur but seldom. In the cantatas in the major mode the most common modulations are the relative minor, the major dominant, the minor supertonic and the major subdominant. Occasionally in a cantata in the major mode there is a change to the parallel minor and with it a modulation to the minor dominant. Only rarely does Luigi use the key of the minor mediant. These are the only modulations in the four groups of cantatas, as far as I have observed; the total tonal range extends no further than the key areas listed here.

As mentioned above, few of the modulations are sustained so that a new tonic is established—each temporary tonic is heard as an embellished degree of the primary tonality. Fluctuation between a given home key and its relative major or minor is characteristic (see, for example, the second unit of *E può soffrirsi*, ex. XV), but it is not as emphatic as in a few of the arie di più parti (*Chi batte, mio core*, for example) where the relative key is almost as prominent as the home key.

It is usual even in the shortest cantatas to find somewhat more modulation in the second unit than in the first. Harmonic activity normally increases in the second unit, which, in all four groups of cantatas, often begins with a movement away from the tonic heard at the close of the first unit, the tonic chord itself usually becoming the pivot.[41] It is taken as dominant of the subdominant initiating a sequence of descending fifths, or it is used as the third degree of the relative minor, and occasionally it is the second degree of the tonality a whole step below. By this increased harmonic activity and by the introduction of new tonal areas in the second unit, the contrast between the two units is enhanced.

Modulations are usually realized through a pivot chord or through a pivot tonality. An example of what I mean by pivot tonality is the movement from B-flat to D minor in the second unit of *Precorrea* (ex. X). The tonic B-flat is taken as pivot chord in the modulation to G minor, but the key of G is the pivot to D minor, for D arrives as the minor dominant of G. The return to B-flat is made again through G minor. The mode of the D chord is changed to major so that it moves back to G, but to G as submediant and not as tonic. The movement to D is terse and of no duration. This constant change from one center to another is characteristic. But the frequent excursions from the primary tonality do not create a strong element of conflict, as I have emphasized above. They are an extension of the ambitus of the tonic, of its sphere of action. The dramatic possibilities of tonality are not yet realized.

Another general tonal characteristic is the tendency before the closing segment of a cantata (the first units of the ternary and rondo cantatas and the second units of the binary and rounded binary) to turn toward the dominant key area. A cadence in the key of the dominant occurs in about one third of the cantatas at this point in the formal designs.[42] Only a little less usual here is a return to the home key with a Phrygian or a semi-cadence on the dominant chord.[43] Within the concluding segment just before the final phrase, a cadence in the dominant key or in the tonic key on the dominant chord is also usual.[44] A cadence in the relative major or relative minor in this place is not nearly as frequent.[45] When it occurs, however, it is because in the particular context, this key rather than the dominant leads more smoothly into the closing passage and affords a desirable major-minor contrast.

Since in both units of the binary and rounded binary cantatas the return to the tonic in the closing segment is usually either prepared by the dominant key area or confirmed by the dominant Phrygian or semi-cadence, the two units frequently share the same penultimate cadence— this is especially true of the rounded binary cantatas where the two units have the same closure.

One other noteworthy characteristic is the importance of the harmonic relationship of the fifth, both in the movement from one chord to another and in the movement from one key to another. Especially in the second units one frequently finds a phrase or two constructed on the descending sequence of fifths, either non-modulating or, less often, modulating. The ascending sequence of fifths occurs less frequently. These sequences, to be sure, are by no means as extensive nor as rhythmically propulsive as they are in later Baroque music, but their quality of generating movement is beginning to make itself felt.

Also normal is the key relationship of the fifth. This is exemplified in the binary cantata *Risolvetevi* (ex. XIII), where the harmonic movement is primarily by fifths, ascending in the first unit, descending in the second. The cantata begins by establishing the home key—C minor; the inner segment of the first unit (measure 9 ff.), after shifting abruptly to the key of the relative major, moves for the most part by ascending fifths in harmonic sequence, each cadential goal relating to the next as a subdominant. Not only is the subdominant relationship stressed, but the goal before the concluding segment is the subdominant (m. 22). In the second unit the descending circle of fifths is heard in three different phrases, with the relationship dominant-tonic, rather than subdominant-tonic, emphasized. This relationship is reaffirmed in the penultimate passage (m. 48 ff.), the passage corresponding to that in the first unit cadencing in the subdominant. Here, preceding the final phrase to the tonic, the cadence is in the key of the minor dominant.

The general tonal characteristics of an arietta corta are illustrated in the binary cantata *Taci, ohime* (ex. XVI). A home key is established in the opening phrase and confirmed in the closing phrase of each of the two units; between these points the tonic, C minor, is avoided. In the first unit the inner phrases cadence in the keys of the relative major and the subdominant; the second unit begins in the home key, but there is no cadence until the relative major is reached. The increased harmonic activity of the second unit is evident in the succeeding movement toward the minor dominant of the relative major, an unusual modulation, especially in this case, for the key is B-flat minor. The concluding segment begins with a further movement away, to E-flat minor, that involves modal mixture. After this the goals are measured by ascending fifths: B-flat, F, C and G minor. (Here B-flat minor is subdominant of the subdominant.) Then, recalling the close of the first unit, the penultimate cadential goal is the relative major (mm. 47-48).

The tonal characteristics of a ternary or rondo cantata are the same as those of the binary or rounded binary, except that the second unit does not always confirm the home key.

Certainly the general tonal characteristics outlined above are evidence of a conscious use of tonality as an element of formal structure.

In the cantatas as a whole, tonality is a factor of movement, variety, contrast, and unity.

The Introductory Passage. Almost without exception the ariette corte begin with a passage that unequivocally asserts the primary tonality. This passage coincides in extent with the first verse, infrequently with two verses; it is one long phrase or a period of two phrases. Only exceptionally is it any longer. The proleptic announcement of the introductory measures by the continuo, a later practice, occurs in only two of the ariette corte, *Addio*, *perfida* and *Ho perso*. In both, the continuo announces the bass of the first phrase.

The introductory passage concludes with a cadence to the tonic (usually an authentic cadence) or, somewhat less frequently, a Phrygian cadence to the dominant. A cadence to any other degree of the tonality, or a modulation, is rare. When two phrases form the introductory segment, usually one phrase cadences to the dominant and the other to the tonic, or both phrases cadence to the same degree, either the tonic or the dominant—the former procedure is more characteristic of the solo cantatas; the latter, of the ensembles.

Occasionally, like a concluding passage, the introductory measures conclude with double cadences to the tonic (see ex. 4a), or with a melismatic prolongation of the cadential passage (see ex. 5a). Common bass patterns are another verification of the relative functions of the two segments: one introduces a tonality, the other reaffirms it.

In about one-sixth of the ariette corte, the introductory segment begins with a motto-like gesture or is itself no more than one.[46] This brief proclamation of the tonality is marked by a pedal (exx. 6a and 7) or cadential bass, often one of the ritornello basses (see exx. 8-10) and by characteristic melodic motives. Among these motives are simple or embellished triadic formations usually composed over a sustained bass tone (ex. 6a); the gentle melodic slide—the "Tancredi" *accento*[47] (exx. 10, XVI); a brief motive rising disjunctly from the dominant to the mediant and descending by a skip of a fourth to the leading tone (ex. XIII);[48] and a similarly terse gesture rising from tonic to mediant and returning to the tonic—the "pupillette" motive that Cesti quotes in his parody cantata *Aspettate* (ex. 11).[49] In *Querelatevi* (ex. 9), where this last mentioned melodic motive introduces the cantata, the contrast in register between the two segments of the opening melodic phrase constitutes a further trait shared by numerous other cantatas.[50] The motto-like gesture is not merely structural, but theatrical. It acts as a curtain-raiser inviting the auditor to collect and focus his attention.

That the quality of movement and melody in these introductory gestures is determined to some degree by the text can be easily seen in some
strophic variations. Although strophic variation does not usually involve
elaborate change, in some instances one finds marked variation to suit the
text situation. For example, the melodic variation in the fourth strophe
of *Ingordo* responds to "caduca" in the verse "Vita caduca e frale"
(ex. 12b). The melismatic opening of the fifth strophe evokes the suggested speed and brightness of its text, "Lampo è l'humana vita!"
(ex. 12c). Compare, too, the introductory gestures of the first and third
strophes of *Perche ratto* (ex. 13a and b). The exclamatory quality of the
former and the statement of fact of the latter are musically contrasted.
(Noteworthy is the resemblance between the opening of the third strophe
of *Perche ratto* (ex. 13b) and the opening of *Ingordo human desio* (ex. 12a)
of which the text is also a declarative statement.)

What was later to become fixed in the *Devise*, a repetition of the
introductory measures, occurs seldom in Luigi's cantatas—in all I have
seen no more than ten examples.[51] Repetition in the form of exact or
inexact sequence is also infrequent. In two of the cantatas where this
occurs (exx. 14 and 16), the sequence at the fifth above (or fourth below)
is in the key of the minor dominant, a modulation that is quite common
in the early part of the first unit. In the third cantata that begins with
sequence (ex. XVIII)—the sequence here comprises a larger two-part
period—the tonal relationship is that of the descending fifth (or ascending
fourth), a relationship that is more frequent in the composition of sequence than that of the ascending fifth. The sequence in this case effects
a return to the tonic key, the modulation to the minor dominant having
occurred within the opening two-part period.

One also finds the tonic-dominant relationship in a kind of asymmetrical sequence that appears at the beginning of several cantatas. It is
the statement-answer type that involves the exchange of the pentachord
tonic-dominant with the tetrachord dominant-tonic, or vice versa (ex. 15;
see also the incipits of exx. VII and XVII).

The distinctive quality of the introductory passage is emphasized in
some of the ariette by metric and tempo contrast with what follows.[52] In
fact, this tendency to set the opening passage apart is the cause of most
of the instances of segmentation in the first unit.

The Envelope Design. Luigi's manner of treating the poetic device,[53]
with which 44 of the ariette corte begin,[54] not only makes evident the
differences between opening and closing passages, but also reveals an
important aspect of his style—the preference for asymmetry in repetition.

Undoubtedly because the essential textual trait of this design is the recurrence of the initial verse at the close of the unit—a return to the beginning—the composer usually retains a semblance of the original setting of the reprise verse when it recurs at the close of the unit. But at the same time he transforms or varies, extends or curtails in order to suit the different musical function of the second setting—its function as closure.

There are as many ways in which Luigi recalls and transforms the original setting as the number of times the design occurs in his cantatas. What is quoted, how much is modified and the means of modification, the length, manner, and place of extension—all these are variables.

Some basic general procedures, however, are evident. The most common is to begin the final passage with a modified or exact quotation from the introductory segment, but to substitute another and more conclusive phrase for the original close.[55] In *Taci, ohime* (ex. XVI), for example, the concluding passage begins by quoting the first phrase of the opening with some rhythmic contraction, then skips two measures and quotes the final segment, which it uses as the beginning of a melismatic closing phrase. The two settings are of the same length, but whereas the first moves to the relative major, the second concludes with an affirmation of the tonic—Luigi never quotes the close of the introductory passage without including or appending a cadence in the tonic.

Another general procedure is to quote the entire introductory passage with harmonic, melodic and/or rhythmic alterations and preface it with a new segment (compare 4a and b), or follow it with a new conclusion (compare 6a and b).[56] In the envelope design of *Mi contento* (ex. XVII), one finds an ingenious modification of this procedure—Luigi composes an entirely new passage using all the material of the original. The setting of the reprise verse at the close of the unit begins with the second member of the sequence from the opening, transposed to the key of the subdominant. Following an abrupt remodulation through V of V, both portions of the sequence are stated in their original order, but redistributed imitatively between continuo and voice, and concluding with a slight alteration for cadential purposes.

In another modification of the second procedure, Luigi omits the opening segment, quoting only the closing phrase and extending it, usually by preceding the quoted segment with a new phrase (compare ex. 17a and b).[57] Quotation of the concluding segment of the first passage without the addition of new measures before or after it also occurs, but it is not as characteristic.[58]

In fact, Luigi generally tends to make the concluding passage longer, not shorter, than the introductory one. Though he usually does this by composing new music preceding or concluding the quoted segment, one also finds instances of extension by repetition. For example, in *M'uccidete* (ex. XVIII), where the phrases of the first setting are rearranged in a new order, one phrase is heard twice more, once transposed to the relative major. As compared to the opening design of a b c b' b' (b' is b transposed down a fourth), the concluding passage is c b' a b b'' b' b' (b'' is b in the key of the relative major).

Less common than the procedures whereby something new is made of the concluding period while quoting some part of the original setting, is the composing of an entirely new closure.[59] Like all other envelope designs, however, those that are composed in this manner consistently retain a metrical and tonal relationship between the two settings of the reprise verse.[60] Especially interesting among these designs are those that recall the opening yet quote nothing. For example, the conclusion of *Ohime, madre* (ex. 18) shares with the introduction its large melodic contour of the gradual descending tonic octave and its final cadential phrase, but Luigi changes the line by inventing a new motive. Instead of the repeated minor second, the descending third is the primary melodic motive of the second line. The new setting is longer than the first, as is usually the case (brackets in the example embrace the minor seconds in the first passage, the thirds in the second passage).

The only procedure not encountered is that of complete identity of the two passages with nothing changed and nothing added. In *Sei pur dolce*, (compare ex. 5a and b), the only cantata where the passages are nearly identical,[61] the differences include rhythmic changes in the first three measures of the melody and harmonic changes in the first three beats. Close to exact quotation is the transposition uniquely employed in *Non mi fate mentire* (ex. XI).

In brief, the usual compositional techniques used in the setting of the envelope design entail the setting of the first verse as an introductory passage, with the conventional traits of such a passage; when the verse recurs at the close of the unit, Luigi finds changes in its setting necessary in order to satisfy the new function of the verse. In the concluding passages one finds more repetition of single words, longer phrases, more frequent use of melismas, of hemiola, and of prolonged cadential gestures—all traits of his final segments. The setting of the reprise verse in the concluding passage, which is most often a combination of previously-heard and newly-composed material, is in large part determined by the function of the passage as conclusion. The context of each individual cantata determines the degree and nature of variations on this basic envelope design.

Phrase Structure. Irregular phrase length is a characteristic of Luigi's music in general. Although phrase lengths do in part depend upon the number of syllables included within them—short phrases tend to have fewer syllables than long ones—they generally reveal no exact correspondence to the meter of the poetry. For example, the ternary cantata *E d'amore* has a text entirely of octosyllables, but the musical setting is formed of phrases of seven different lengths.

In most cantatas phrase lengths only occasionally correlate with verse lengths; there are some, however, in which the asymmetry of irregular phrasing is juxtaposed to the relatively exact symmetry of a succession of phrases of equal length. In the rondo *Deh, soccori,* for example, the uniform octosyllables of the first unit are set to four phrases of different length: nine, five, ten and 12 measures, respectively; but the second unit, whose text is also formed of octosyllables, has a different structure. Here, except for the first exceptionally long period combining the first and second couplets, we find a succession of rhythmically identical or nearly identical phrases, each the setting of one octosyllable. The rhythmic pattern is first presented at the close of the long opening period, with the fourth verse. Thereafter, each of the succeeding four verses and also the repetition of each of the last two verses is sung to the same rhythm—a total of seven statements of the rhythmic phrase. Thus, following the opening period of 17 measures, there are three nearly identical periods, each composed of two symmetrical four-measure phrases, except for the last, which concludes with a five-measure phrase that is similar to the others but for the extension of its last two syllables. In cantatas like *Deh, soccori,* where one finds this kind of juxtaposition, the practice of setting uniform verses to phrases of equal length and similar rhythmic pattern usually does not extend beyond portions of individual units.[62] Cantatas like *Amor, e perche* (ex. XII), in which most of the phrases are formed of a recurring rhythmic pattern—varied, to be sure, but not departing from the metrical framework, and correlated with verses of equal length— are not common.[63] This small group of ariette, all of whose texts are entirely of hexasyllables or octosyllables, are rhythmically organized in a way that recalls the songs and dances of the generation preceding Rossi's. In these cantatas, as in the earlier monodies, certain types of musical rhythms are combined with certain types of Italian verse; the rhythmic patterns that recur are, in fact, among the common ones found in the earlier repertory. Of the characteristic rhythm patterns defined by Putnam Aldrich in his monograph,[64] those that Luigi continues to use are found among the "ottonario" rhythms—the corrente rhythm of four triple beats,[65] the hemiola rhythm,[66] which he usually alternates with the corrente pattern, and the rhythm of four slow duple beats.[67] Among Aldrich's "senario" rhythms Luigi employs the corrente rhythm of four triple beats to each pair of hexasyllables.[68] The phrasing in this small group of pieces that are characterized by their rhythmic symmetry is by no means representative of Luigi's characteristic style.

What one finds in the majority of cantatas is a frequent lack of correspondence between phrase lengths and poetic design, a feature that is in part due to the fact that some phrases comprise two verses, others one; in addition, pairs of verses combined into a single phrase may be either equal or unequal in length. For example, the four unequal phrases that form the second unit of *Il contento* (ex. XIX) are (1) a couplet of heptasyllables, (2) a single hendecasyllable, and (3) and (4) two pairings of a heptasyllable and an hendecasyllable. The longest phrases, the third and fourth, are those with the largest number of syllables; the shortest, the second, is the phrase with the fewest. As against this superficial correspondence, however, other factors of rhythm and syllabification (particularly the employment of melismas) are far more instrumental in determining phrase length. This is particularly evident in the comparison of the third and fourth phrases of *Il contento*'s second unit.

Another idiosyncrasy of phrase structure is its flowing freedom. Unsegmented single phrases,[69] long or short, freely alternate with periods formed of two or three or even four segments. One sees in the cantata *Lungi da me* (ex. XX), for example, the wide variation in the degree of phrase segmentation that is characteristic of Luigi's music in general. Throughout the cantata we find not only constantly changing phrase lengths,[70] but a variety of kinds of phrases and different degrees of relationship among them. The two two-part phrases (mm. 42-50, 69-74), for example, each of which occurs between phrases of different structure, are both composed of equal segments; but in one case (mm. 69-74) these segments are related sequentially, whereas in the other (mm. 42-50) they are not. The four three-part phrases, only two of which are consecutive, are all composed of two segments of equal or nearly equal length and a longer cadential segment, but they are organized differently. In two of these phrases the first two segments are related by a partial rhythmic sequence (mm. 11-19, 23-31); in the third (mm. 60-69), the second segment is a more exact overall sequence of the preceding segment (mm. 60-69); and in the fourth (mm. 1-10), where the three-part structure is articulated only in the vocal line, the non-sequential second segment answers the basic semitone motive of the motto: C-B-C with its inversion on the dominant: G-A-flat-G. Like the three-part phrases, the one four-part phrase (mm. 81-89) begins with segments of equal length, the first two of which are sequential, and concludes with a longer cadential gesture. Typically this climactic phrase, the longest of the cantata, is its concluding passage. Interspersed among these subdivided phrases are five seamless or near-seamless phrases whose lengths range from 3⅓ to 9⅓ measures.

The closest relationship among phrases is found in measures 11-31 of the first unit. The final phrase of this unit begins (m. 23) as a transposition of the second phrase (m. 11) at the fourth below (with slight changes in the bass), but deviates in the penultimate measure of the third segment so that the unit concludes with a quotation of the original voice cadence at pitch—in the tonic key rather than in the key of the minor dominant, where the period would have led if the transposition had been maintained. Between these two phrases is a short one that sets the key-displacement in motion by introducing a sequence of the last segment of the preceding phrase. No succession of phrases in the second unit is related in exactly this manner. Although the internal sequence that forms the first two segments of the final phrase is derived from the phrase beginning in measure 69, the two differ in structure. Equally dissimilar are the other two phrases that are closely related thematically. The one beginning in measure 51 starts as a sequence of the preceding phrase (mm. 43-50), but the sequence is altered. While retaining the progression of descending fifths—B-flat, E-flat, A-flat, d, G and c, the first time (ex. 19a), and g, C, f, B-flat, E-flat, A-flat, d, G and c, the second time (ex. 19b)—Luigi displaces the chords rhythmically so that the seventh chord in first inversion is no longer an upbeat but a downbeat (the figuration below the bass lines in ex. 19 is my addition). Extending the sequence beyond the fourth measure, the composer also avoids the clear two-part division of the preceding phrase.

As observed in *Lungi da me*, a characteristic of the three-part period is the sequential relationship of the first two segments and the cadential quality of the third, longer segment. The Rossian period of two segments, on the other hand, is not composed in any consistent manner. The two segments may be of the same or of different length; one may be syllabic, the other melismatic; one sequential, the other cadential. In general, however, the two parts are related in some ways and contrasted in others. The two phrases may be related rhythmically and contrasted in their tonal goals and melodic range; they may be related by partial sequence or partial repetition and contrasted in their different cadence dispositions; they may be related harmonically and contrasted in their melodic contours.

Sequential relationships within a period and between one period or single phrase and another are characteristic of Luigi's music in general. But they are not usually present unless there is text repetition.[71] In fact, in the ternary and rondo second units where there is little or no text repetition, there is often no use of sequence at all.[72] In such situations phrase interrelations are confined to those characteristic of the repertoire as a whole: occasional common rhythmic and melodic motives, phrase-bridging progressions governed by a stable harmonic rhythm, and recurrent cadential gestures.

The extent of the use of sequence varies from cantata to cantata, but in general one finds sequential procedures used not more than two to four times within an arietta corta. Sequence is not normally a primary means of thematic integration and expansion.[73] Typical for the amount and kind of sequence in them are *E può soffrirsi* (ex. XV), *Se nell' arsura* (ex. 1), *Lungi da me* (ex. XX), and *Taci, ohime* (ex. XVI).[74]

In relating two phrases sequentially Luigi usually begins with a clear quotation at another tonal level, but quickly introduces changes of rhythmic and/or melodic details and makes tonal alterations that normally lead the second phrase to a free and new conclusion (ex. XXI, compare mm. 29-33 and 33-36). Changes in the intervallic relationship of the sequence (quite apart from those introduced for purely tonal reasons) are quite common (exx. 20 and 21a). The composer even abandons the sequence for a measure or two, then returns to it (ex. 21b). Characteristics of large-scale sequences of this kind, evident in the examples cited, are the close adherence of the second phrase to the rhythm of the model phrase and the new relationships between the vocal and bass lines with the latter frequently participating only partially in the sequence.

Exact or nearly exact melodic-rhythmic-harmonic sequence such as forms the close of the first unit of *Precorrea* (ex. X) is rare.[75] The pairing of entire phrases by literal transposition to a different tonal level is prominent in the cantatas of the next generation of composers, but occurs only sporadically in Luigi's music.

Occurring more frequently than the large-scale sequence described above, which involves entire phrases and is a means of forming large periods and of extending a unit in length, is sequence on a smaller, motive-level, scale, within the phrase. One variety of this small-scale sequential activity, like the large-scale sequence, is normally associated with text repetition. This involves the sequential relationship of two or more distinct segments of a phrase. As mentioned earlier and as demonstrated in *Lungi da me* (ex. XX), phrases formed of several segments are often partially sequential. In such sequences the symmetrical involvement of all three elements—melody, rhythm and harmony—is as frequent as an asymmetrical realization in which one or two of the elements are altered.[76] The exactness or inexactness of the sequence is invariably the result of tonal considerations (as it is, to be sure, in large-scale sequence), alterations being made to maintain coherence of key and harmonic direction (see exx. 22 and 23).

Small-scale sequences do not necessarily form distinct segments of a phrase; they also merge with free initial and/or cadential gestures. The successive repetition of a melodic figure or of a harmonic progression at different pitch levels—the two may be and are often, but not always, combined—is a frequent concomitant of melismatic passages. Within a melisma a motive is usually sequentially repeated no more than one or two times, only rarely three or more times. The sequence is most frequently at the interval of a descending or ascending second. When the bass line accompanying the melodic sequence is also sequentially composed, it normally supports the first tones of the melodic motive and its sequential repetitions at the tenth below (see ex. II, mm. 8-9, 78-79; ex. III, mm. 15-18, 33-35; ex. VI, mm. 19-20). When the bass line is free of the melodic sequence it is sometimes composed in contrary motion to it (ex. XV, mm. 28-29 and ex. XXIII, mm. 45-48), but more often it has no particular contrapuntal relationship to the sequential ascending or descending vocal line, being harmonic in character (see ex. XV, mm. 6-7; ex. XVI, mm. 37-38; ex. V, mm. 15-16, 31-34). One also finds melodic sequence within a melisma supported by a sustained bass tone (ex. II, second half of m. 79; ex. XVI, m. 19 and m. 49).

The most common harmonic sequences at the motive level are those in which the progression of chord roots is either of descending fifths or of descending diatonic seconds. When the chord roots descend by fifth, the bass either presents the successive chord roots (ex. XII, mm. 38-40, 43-45; ex. XVIII, mm. 2-5) or alternates a chord root with a chord third (ex. XXI, mm. 27-28; ex. XXVII, mm. 94-101), occasionally adding the passing seventh of the first chord between them (ex. XX, mm. 44-45, 51-55; ex. 20, mm. 2-3). The vocal line generally alternates the fifth and the third of the successive chords when the chord roots are in the bass, and moves in contrary motion to the bass from the third of one chord to the root of the next when the root and the third of the chords are alternated in the bass. The realizations are traditional. The descending scale bass is most often found with a vocal line that moves in parallel tenths with it (ex. X, mm. 4-7; ex. XXI, mm. 13-18).[77] Occasionally one finds the suspension 7-6 in the vocal line (ex. V, mm. 12-14; ex. 21b, first phrase), but only rarely the suspension 4-3 (ex. 21b, second phrase). The bass is normally left unfigured, its realization dependent upon the knowledge of the continuo player. In most instances the scale line can be realized with 5-6 or 7-6 over each bass tone (if 7-6 is chosen, the first bass tone of the descending scale should be realized with 5-6 in order to prepare the seventh that follows). Should the harmonic rhythm suggest avoiding division of the bass tones, then the descending line may be interpreted as the alternation of the chord root, chord third (ex. IX, mm. 2-3, the figuration in parentheses is my addition).

Much less frequent than either the sequence of descending fifths or of descending seconds is the sequential progression whose bass tones move in ascending diatonic or chromatic seconds. The ascending diatonic scale is realized like its inversion—with parallel tenths in the melodic line and with 5-6 or 7-6 over each bass tone (ex. XVI, mm. 7-10; ex. XX, mm. 81-85; ex. XXI, mm. 30-31, 34-35). The ascending chromatic scale, however, has other harmonic implications. Here the progression of chord roots ascends a perfect fourth and descends a minor third—basically a stepwise progression of chords each of which is embellished by its dominant (ex. XXVII, mm. 105-110).

As the examples cited demonstrate, sequence on a motivic level rarely forms all of a phrase (except for its final V-I cadence). In general a sequence initiates a phrase, forms a major part of it and leads to a free cadential segment. Sequence is initiated in the central portion of a phrase only occasionally. In the introductory passage of *Hor guardate* (ex. IX), for example, the sequential measure activitates harmonic movement after the static motto opening; in *Respira* (ex. V, mm. 12-14), the sequence serves to continue and increase momentum in an unusually long phrase. Whenever they occur, small-scale sequences give breadth and length to a phrase and also normally generate harmonic activity.

Recitative. Recitative is relatively infrequent in the ariette corte; it occurs in above one fourth of the rounded binary and ternary cantatas, in a smaller proportion of the rondos and in a larger proportion of the simple binary pieces. None of the ariette is composed in recitative from beginning to end,[78] and few have an entire unit in recitative. Generally recitative forms a segment of one of the two units, much more frequently the second than the first.

The recitative passage is usually transitional or introductory. In the binary cantatas, where it is largely confined to the second unit, a recitative passage often leads to the concluding segment of the cantata, a movement in aria. The rounded binary cantatas, on the other hand, are distinguished by the fact that recitative is largely absent from the second unit—it occurs in only two cantatas of the group.[79] In the ternary and rondo cantatas the recitative is usually at the beginning or at the end of the second unit. An exception is *Non c'è che dire* where the recitative is contained within the second unit in the manner of the simple binary pieces—the second unit in this cantata, in fact, is a simple binary arietta.

In the cantatas composed entirely in duple meter, recitative is usually no more frequent than in the rest of the cantatas. The quality of movement is primarily aria, or rhapsodic declamation, as in *Gelosia* and *Precorrea* (ex. X).

Recitative passages are almost invariably settings of *impari* verses, usually heptasyllables or hendecasyllables—verses in which the binary cantatas, above any of the other three groups, abound. As mentioned earlier, it is in these passages that the text is best served. In the recitatives the text's rhythmic, sonorous values are perfectly inflected, its meanings and moods are interpreted in appropriate musical gestures. The quality of the recitative is invariably influenced by the nature of the verses. In *Udite, amanti*, for example, the transitional recitative passage is *concitato* because of the words "a battaglia mortale!"; in *Se dolente* it is a dramatic declamation that fits the words "Taci, misero, e mori!"; in *Occhi belli, occhi miei* the transitional recitative passage, which occurs with the verse "Ma lasso, e che diss'io," a pathetic exclamation borrowed from the laments, where it usually marks a change of mood and also articulates the structure, is an austere utterance.

In most of the ariette corte recitative is a means of contrast—it sets lyrical aria passages in relief, it articulates the longer second units, it is a means of attaining the flexible segmentary character most evident in the binary cantatas where it appears more than in any other group.

Not surprisingly, Luigi's manner of composing recitative has few if any idiosyncrasies that might set it apart from the style of his generation at large. The characteristic recitative earmarks are there: sustained bass tones, a harmonic rhythm noticeably slower than that of the arias, a vocal part markedly more responsive to syllable length and lacking the unifying melodic motives, regularly recurring rhythmic patterns and periodized phrase structure of aria-style writing. One notes with interest the presence of devices that look backward to the Monteverdi generation rather than forward to Cesti and Stradella. Major-minor contrast, for instance, still occurs occasionally between the closing chord of a phrase and the first chord of the succeeding one, both having the same root. The change is usually realized melodically by the leap of a minor sixth, from the third of the major to the root of the minor tonic (ex. XIX, fifth measure) or from the fifth of a dominant chord to the third of its minor counterpart, effecting a change of implied tonic (ex. 24). The ascending échappée is also heard (ex. XIX, the last sixteenth of measure 3 to the first quarter of measure 4), but does not prevail as in earlier Baroque recitatives. Within an extended segment of recitative the interpolation of a melismatic passage is characteristic. Frequently, too, an arioso or melismatic cadence concludes a recitative. Of the harmonic and contrapuntal licenses of early operatic recitative, however, there is no trace: dissonance is largely confined to conventional cadence figures, where it invariably receives orthodox preparation and resolution.

Recitative is generally composed for solo voice, but there are successful realizations of the recitative style for two voices in the ensembles. In these passages the two voices sing both together—usually in thirds and sixths—and in alternation, one voice silent or sustaining a tone while the other voice repeats or continues the text. Except for the relative infrequency of close imitation, the compositional techniques are those found in Monteverdi's madrigals for two and three voices in Books VII-IX. In the Rossi ensembles, to be sure, as in the ariette corte for solo voice, aria-style predominates; recitative occurs only occasionally and then usually forms but a small part of the cantata.

Some Cadential Types. The cadential types discussed here—the prolongation cadences, the ritornelli and the migrating cadential formula "Speranza"—are those that recur in many cantatas with the same particular functions and with identifiable traits. They thus represent a kind of cross-section of the total range of cadential possibilities, but one limited to particular formulas as opposed to general types. For example, many of the patterns discussed below form subgroups of the general category of double cadences (i.e., those employing any cadential movement to the tonic and its exact or free repetition); but it is their recognizable, distinct features that are under discussion here.

The prolongation cadences, which are distinguished from the typical inner cadences of a few beats by their expansive, theatrical quality, are found in most of Luigi's cantatas.[80] Their identifying feature is the postponement of the dominant's resolution to the tonic. The cadences appear consistently with metric and melodic variants, but their bass line is immediately recognizable. With numbers representing the degrees of the scale, the basic pattern of the bass line is: 4 5 6 4 5 1. Other related patterns that appear frequently are 5 4 5 4 5 1, 3 4 5 6 4 5 1, 6 4 5 6 4 5 1 and 4 5 3 4 5 6 4 5 1. While the bass line indicates the presence of prolongation, only the harmonic articulation, which is in part the result of the melodic line, defines the particular kind of prolongation.

The first of the three basic types is purely ornamental prolongation.[81] Either the tonic $^6_4$ chord or the dominant is embellished by various states of the subdominant or supertonic chord before resolving. The embellishing chords are formed almost fortuitously over the auxiliaries of the dominant; they are the result of linear movement in both parts. Among the more frequent dissonances, actual or implied, are the sevenths of the supertonic or subdominant chords. Only occasionally does one hear the chord of the submediant. The sixth degree in the bass tends to act as appoggiatura to the dominant, but its resolution is postponed by the sub-dominant auxiliary (exx. 25, 26 and 28b).[82]

The second type of prolongation cadence is distinguished by the greater rhythmic-harmonic emphasis placed on the initial appearance of the dominant chord. Whereas in the previous examples the dominant is first heard only briefly or in passing, here it forms a moment of pronounced arrival prior to the continuation of the phrase with embellishing, prolonging subdominant chords. Movement towards the final goal begins only after the dominant's arrival. With the embellishing chords momentum increases and the phrase moves forward past the second dominant to the tonic (exx. 27a, 28a).[83] Three occurrences of the dominant, as in the concluding phrase of *Son divenuto* (ex. 27b), result in an even greater extension of movement, but are rare.

The deceptive progression marks the third kind of prolongation cadence, which occurs less frequently than the others.[84] The phrase moves past the first dominant to the submediant where it pauses on the chord of that degree. The submediant has authentic chordal significance in this cadence and is not an auxiliary as in the first and second types of prolongation (ex. 29).

In some closing passages we find two types of prolongation. At the close of *Sempre dunque* (ex. 29) the sequential melismatic movement that extends the third type of prolongation leads via iii and IV to the dominant; following it the submediant and subdominant degrees embellish the gesture that leads at last to the final cadence.[85]

When a prolongation cadence recurs in a cantata, it usually appears with a new melodic and rhythmic realization. Both units of *Son divenuto*, for example, close with a prolongation cadence of the second type (ex. 27a and b). Although the close of the first unit is not extended like that of the second, the basic cadential progression of both cadences is essentially the same. The recurrence of the third type of prolongation that relates the closing passages of the two units of *E può soffrirsi* (ex.XV) is especially noteworthy, for the deceptive progression, as I mentioned before, is not frequent in Luigi's cantatas. Here, uniquely, it occurs twice in both passages. The juxtaposition of the major and minor modes in the final passage is also unusual. This particular event seems to respond to the text, for striking examples of similar major-minor contrasts occur in other cantatas with the mention of "morire."[86]

The ritornelli are distinguished by their compactness and their traditional bass melodies. They are brief cadential phrases for the continuo alone (in the ariette corte no other instrumental parts are required), occurring generally at the close of a unit and infrequently within a unit.[87] In the arie di più parti and laments they most often follow a recurring inner refrain. Although a ritornello may recur in a cantata, such recurrence is clearly not an inseparable part of its function; there are a few cantatas where a ritornello is heard but once.[88] The ritornelli do not appear as introductory passages in Luigi's cantatas, although many opening gestures are based on their bass patterns.

A ritornello is found more frequently at the close of a rondo refrain than anywhere else in the ariette corte—it rarely occurs in a binary cantata, and is notated only infrequently in a rounded binary or ternary cantata.[89] In the rondo and ternary cantatas the ritornello is never used at the close of the second unit, since this leads directly to the recapitulation of the first unit; but in a few binary cantatas where it occurs, the ritornello is used at the close of either or both units.[90] Of the three rounded binary cantatas notated with ritornello, one places it only at the end of the first unit; another, at the close of both, and the third, at the close of both but not at the close of the last strophic variation of the second unit. Despite the fact that the ritornello appears at the close of six binary pieces and one rounded binary, and at the close of the final statement of three rondo refrains, it seems that as a regular practice the ritornello was omitted at the end of a cantata. The scores, at least, only rarely notate a ritornello with the last appearance of a recurring (and concluding) unit such as a rondo refrain, even though in each of its previous statements that unit is concluded by a ritornello. Thus it may be that even in those binary and rounded binary cantatas whose second unit is notated with a ritornello, it was omitted in the final strophic repetition. This is not clear in the sources, for usually only texts of the strophic repetitions are given and no other rubrics.[91] Some light is shed by the fact that sometimes in place of the ritornello in the last appearance of the recurring unit that originally ended with one, the final passage is extended by the addition of another phrase for voice and bass, or prolonged by the insertion of a melisma (as at the close of the last statement of the refrain of *Ferma, Giove*, ex. 30). More often, however, nothing takes the place of the omitted instrumental cadence. If our interpretation is correct, the ritornello's role in such cases is exclusively interlinear: it gives pause to the voice, permitting it a short respite before the next section. This function is unnecessary at the end of the cantata.

The continuo cadence invariably reaffirms the tonal goal of the phrase it follows, and in all but one cantata it conforms metrically to the unit to which it is appended.[92] In the binary cantata *Se nell'arsura* (ex. I), whose two units differ metrically, the ritornello that concludes the second unit, though functionally identical to its predecessor, has a different metric structure. The ritornello is in essence a reiterated cadence[93] and, in fact, in a few cantatas its bass is the same as that of the preceding cadence.

There are various ways in which the sources notate the final tone of the vocal line when a ritornello follows it; the concordances for one cantata do not consistently agree. In one source the voice may sustain its closing tone for the entire length of the ritornello with the tone exactly measured; in another, the final tone is sustained for the initial part of the ritornello, the duration of the first chord, followed by rests, and in yet another the final tone may be written as a breve with a fermata followed by no rest. This last manner of notating the close of the vocal line is the most common and seems to imply that regularly the voice sustained its tone as long as it could for the duration of the ritornello—until its end, if possible.

A ritornello in Luigi's cantatas is generally represented by a simple notated bass line with no indication of the upper parts.[94] Occasionally the rubric "ritornello" alone appears, requiring that a cadential passage be improvised. Only infrequently are this rubric and a bass line notated together. Once in Luigi's cantatas, at the close of *Al cenno*, "ritornello" is replaced by "Chiaccona."[95] This designation accompanies a written-out continuo cadence in which the bass is, in fact, a traditional ciaccona soggetto repeated once (ex. 31).[96] Although it is not used in any of Luigi's cantatas, the rubric "Passacaglio" (ex. 32)[97]—or "Passacaglie,"[98] "Passagallo,"[99] "Passagaglio" (exx. 33, 34)[100]—designates a ritornello in a number of cantata MSS. The ritornelli in Luigi's cantatas and in those of his contemporaries are, in fact, for the most part variants of the passacaglia bass formulae. Most frequent among these is the pattern appearing at the close of the refrain of *Hor guardate* (ex. IX) and in examples 6b (below, p. 138), 30, 35, VI and XXII; it has been identified as one of the principal passacaglia bass formulae.[101] Another frequently heard design, one called "neutral" by Richard Hudson,[102] is associated with neither the passacaglia nor the ciaccona, but like them was also used in Baroque instrumental ostinato compositions (exx. 36 and I). In Luigi's cantatas and in those of his contemporaries these formulae generally follow a cadence for voice and continuo that concludes with the progression V-I. A ritornello that follows a Phrygian cadence normally reaffirms that cadence. In each of the ten cantatas by Luigi where a ritornello follows a Phrygian cadence, its bass is the embellished or unembellished descending Phrygian tetrachord—the penultimate tone of the ritornello bass descends a minor second to the root of the final chord (see ex. 37).[103]

Because the MS sources are inconsistent in the inclusion of either a ritornello bass line or a prescriptive rubric, and usually omit both, the question arises: should a ritornello not be improvised more often than the MSS indicate? Perhaps the inconsistency in the MSS is in part due to the particular nature of the ritornello in this repertory. Since it was a cadential formula that could be easily improvised, its notation may have been considered unnecessary. If this was in fact the case, it did not remain so for long: rubrics for the performance of ritornelli appear consistently in cantatas by Caproli and his generation although these are based on the same cadential formulae. Perhaps the solution to this problem may be found through bibliographical investigation. It is conceivable that the copyists of the MSS dating after those in which most of Luigi's cantatas are found were merely more careful in notating ritornelli and prescriptive rubrics. Assuming the possibility that a ritornello was performed even though not specifically prescribed, one must consider where the ritornello would normally occur if improvised. Certainly the ritornelli that are notated offer an answer—they occur at the close of both the units of the binary and rounded binary cantatas and at the close of rondo and ternary first unit. Because of the frequent omission of the continuo cadence after the last occurrence of the rondo and ternary first unit, the ritornello should be added here only if the final segment requires a more conclusive ending. If it is already extended by double cadences and/or by prolonged melismatic movement, the ritornello is probably unnecessary.

Another recurring cadential gesture, found in quite a number of Luigi's cantatas,[104] is identified by both melodic and bass lines. This cadence, which will be called the "Speranza" cadence simply because I became aware of its nature as a migrating cadence in the cantata *Speranza al tuo pallore*, is usually composed in triple meter and in the minor mode.[105] In most cases it is used to set the last five syllables of the final verse of a unit. The upper melodic line is characterized by the basic succession of tones 6 7 5 1 1 7 1 (the numbers represent the degrees of the ascending melodic minor scale). Either the tonic or the second degree occasionally substitutes for the sixth degree at the beginning of the cadence and the penultimate tone is sometimes embellished (exx. 38-44). The bass line usually describes the harmonic progression IV-V-I. In its embellished versions the variants mostly involve some form of subdominant harmony employing the upper auxiliary tones of the dominant; the overall result is simply to intensify the dominant activity (exx. 40, 42a, 43, 44b).

More than half the "Speranza" cadences are composed for two or more voices and thus include a third line. The latter undergoes more variation in detail in its opening than the other parts (compare exx. 38, 39, 40, 44). The rich variety of inflections and harmonic relationships, ornamental and structural, which result because of the slight changes in the third part, are another indication of Luigi's predilection for subtle transformation.

Migrating "Themes." In the cantatas of Luigi and his contemporaries one finds a few specific motives and motive-groupings adapted to verses of a certain number of syllables—hexasyllables, octosyllables and heptasyllables. Because the recurrence of these motives in a substantial number of cantatas gives them quasi-thematic status I refer to them as themes and migrating melodies, but the use of these terms "theme" and "migrating melody" throughout the following discussion is no more than an arbitary convenience. So far as I have determined, there are two identifiable melodies associated with hexasyllables, one with octosyllables, and one with heptasyllables. These recurrent themes are generally placed at the opening of the section in which they occur. The octosyllable theme, however, is heard almost as often in an inner phrase.

One hexasyllable melody, which for purposes of identification I call the "All'armi, mio core!" melody, is composed of two balancing phrases: the first of the pair of phrases begins with the repeated tonic degree preceded by an anacrusis on the lower dominant; it then either remains on the tonic for a total of five syllables, or rises by step to the mediant before returning to the tonic for the final syllable of the line. The answering phrase continues the upward motion to the dominant degree, either by direct leap or via the intervening mediant, to which it may also return after reaching the apex of the phrase (exx. 45-48). In a variant of this theme the two phrases are reversed: the pentachord (tonic-dominant) precedes the tetrachord (dominant-tonic) (see ex. 49).

As the quoted examples might suggest, the theme is frequently found in B-flat major and 6/8 meter. The bass is either the tonic pedal or a ritornello-like design. The phrase length and metrical placement shown in the examples are typical of most of the theme's appearances. The dotted-note rhythm seen in examples III and VI does not appear consistently in this location; its use and placement depend on the length of the syllables. In *Difenditi, amore*, for example, the second tone is dotted because of the length of the syllable and its accent, whereas in *Uscite di porto* the third tone is dotted because the short unaccented syllable after it requires a strong upbeat quality.

Both the contrast of register within an octave span—a trait of Luigi's melodic style mentioned earlier in connection with introductory gestures (above, p. 60)—and the juxtaposition of tetrachord and pentachord are also prominent in the second hexasyllable melody, one I shall call the "Sperate" theme (exx. 50-53).[106] Here, however, the direction of initial movement is the reverse of that found in the "All'armi" theme. The first part of the "Sperate" theme descends through the broken tonic triad, from fifth to root, with rhythmic thesis on the third degree; the second motive outlines the upper descending tetrachord, with arsic tonic and thetic leading tone followed by a leap to the fifth degree—a tonal answer to the first motive. Although it generally occurs with hexasyllables, there are also examples of the theme with three repeated syllables.

The melodic characteristics of the "Sperate" theme make its harmonization tonic-dominant virtually inevitable. Mostly it is notated in 6/2 and 6/4, but there are examples in 6/8. Only three of the examples known to me are in duple meter. Like the "All'armi" melody, this theme occurs primarily at the beginning of a unit.

Of the several variants of the theme that occur in Luigi's cantatas, one makes of the second motive a real rather than a tonal answer and involves a corresponding harmonic change. The progression ascends a fourth from tonic to subdominant (ex. 54) or from dominant to tonic (ex. 55).[107] Another harmonic variant leads the phrase from the minor tonic to its relative major; the minor dominant replacing the usual major is used as mediant of the relative major (ex. 56).[108] In still another variant of the "Sperate" theme, the melody is used as a cadential motive with a Phrygian progression to the dominant (ex. 57a).[109] Besides this occurrence of the motive within the solo strophe of *Mortale, che pensi*, the melody is heard in the opening phrase of the refrain, where it is again realized with a Phrygian cadence (ex. 57b; the basic melody drawn from the two soprano lines is shown in ex. 57c).

In *Uscite di porto*, where it closes the opening period (ex. VI, mm. 7-8), the "Sperate" theme is varied melodically and harmonically as the head of a brief melismatic passage. Its recurrence in the envelope setting at the close of the same unit is preceded by a proleptic announcement of the second motive of the theme, varied, but definitely suggestive of it (ex. VI, mm. 18-21).

Like the two hexasyllable themes, the third migrating melody, a melody associated with octosyllables, is formed sequentially. The features of this recurring theme, which I have termed the "Adorate" melody from its appearance in *Adorate mie catene* (ex. 58), are duple meter, a stepwise descending sequence of falling melodic fifths, and imitative participation of the bass in the sequential pattern. The frequency of bass-soprano imitation is doubtless accounted for by the pairing of descending fifths with ascending fourths in the melody, a combination that can be neatly bridged over by delayed entry at the fifth below or fourth above (exx. 59, 60, 61). Even where outright imitation is lacking between bass and upper voice, the former outlines the root movement by fifths from which the melody itself obviously springs (see especially ex. 62). The melodic skip from third to root of the chord, characteristic of the theme in most of its appearances, is sometimes omitted (ex. 63, bass; ex. 64b, voice) or filled in by stepwise motion (exx. 63, 64b, 66, bass; ex. 62, voices).[110]

The triple meter found in examples 61 and 62 is comparatively rare, as is the melismatic employment of the melody seen in examples 62 and 65. Rarer still is the extent of the theme in *Perche chieder*, where it spans 11 chords through a circle of fifths (ex. 63). In its other appearances the basic four-note motive is usually heard no more than twice in succession in one voice.

Even though I have located it in only six of Luigi's cantatas, a fourth melodic type deserves mention here because of its prominence in all but one of the pieces in which it occurs—most especially in *Non mi fate* (ex. XI), after which I have named it. The melody is associated with verses of seven or six syllables,[111] the first five of which are set as a long anacrusis of five quarter-notes in a meter that is usually notated as 3/2, but whose rhythmic groupings are predominantly those of the modern 6/4. These five notes descend stepwise from the fifth degree to the tonic, from which point the phrase proceeds either by step to the leading-tone (exx. XI, 70) or by leap back to the dominant (exx. XXII, 67-69) as its thetic goal. The choice between these two melodic gestures is obviously dependent on the bass movement. When the bass rises from the tonic by step to the dominant tone, the melody descends a sixth in contrary motion; when the bass moves from the tonic down a step to the leading tone, the melodic line avoids the duplication of the leading tone by skipping up to the dominant. Unlike the other migrating melodies this one does not contain an internal sequence. It is, however, repeated sequentially in *Non mi fate* (ex. XI, mm. 18 ff.) and repeated by imitation between bass and soprano in *A tanti sospiri* and *S'io son vinto* (exx. 67, 68).

It will be noted that the phrase is equally at home in both major and minor. The few variants that appear in its recurrences are harmonic. One is the substitution of the minor chord in place of the major dominant (ex. 68). Another is the movement dominant-dominant passing through the chord of the submediant or through the tonic (exx. 67, 69).

The "Non mi fate" melody is, like the other recurring themes, usually an introductory gesture: in all but one of the cantatas where it occurs it either begins a unit or begins the concluding segment of one. In the rounded binary cantata *Non mi fate* and in the rounded binary arietta with which the aria di più parti *Torna indietro* begins (ex. XXII) it forms the introductory and concluding passages of the first unit and also the final passage of the second; in the binary cantatas *A tanti sospiri* and *S'io son vinto* it begins the concluding segment of the second unit of which it is the primary motive. In *Tenti*, another binary arietta, it also occurs in the concluding segment, but only as a brief appendage in the penultimate phrase, serving to link two statements of the ostinato bass pattern (ex. 69). Its "thematic" character here is admittedly open to question; it is noteworthy, however, that in the strophic variations of this cantata the motive recurs in the same place. Finally, in the rondo *Cor dolente* the theme appears at the beginning of the second unit. Only one source of the duet, however, gives an unembellished version of the theme (*I* Bc, Q 48); in the other sources the characteristic quality is somewhat lost because of the changes (ex. 70b).

Strophic Variation. Only 36 of the ariette corte are strophic variations: 23 binary cantatas, 12 rondos and one rounded binary.[112] The procedures of variation are similar in all three types; there is, however, a difference in application. In the rondos, the variation process is usually limited to the second unit or a part of it, while the first unit-refrain remains unchanged;[113] whereas in the binary cantatas strophic change is not limited to any one unit, but can occur in both. In the one rounded binary cantata that undergoes strophic variation, *Uscite di porto*, Luigi varies only the reprise conclusion of the second unit's strophic repetitions, thus emphasizing the segment of the cantata that distinguishes its particular formal design. Because of this feature, *Uscite di porto* is not included in the following remarks, but is discussed separately in the chapter dealing with the traits of the rounded binary design.

In most of the cantatas where it is employed, the strophic variation procedure entails no more than a few melodic embellishments, some rhythmic changes, and an occasional contraction or expansion of a phrase accompanied by changes in the bass line; the original setting is rarely extensively or radically changed. Indeed, in a majority of cases many of the phrases of the original vocal line remain untouched while a few undergo slight melodic alteration, much of it motivated primarily by the need to accommodate the syllable lengths and accents of the new text. The more substantial divergences range from the extension of a phrase by a melismatic insertion, to the creation of an entirely new phrase. On the whole, however, variation in Luigi's cantatas is less a matter of accretion than of revision.

Interestingly enough, this procedure is most consistently applied in Luigi's bass lines; rare is the cantata unit in which he does not quote the bass with some changes. A shift of accent, a hemiola in place of the usual division, the insertion of passing tones, the omission of a few tones, neighbor-note embellishment, the substitution of a pedal for a moving line, change of octave, an inverted order of notes, augmentation, diminution— these regularly take place with or without variation in the melodic line.

It is notable that half of the rondos that incur variation are composed with an ostinato bass; the unit or segment that is strophically varied in these cantatas is itself composed of melodic variations on a repeated bass pattern.[114] True to the character of ostinato compositions, the variation in these cantatas is more consistently confined to the upper voice. The divisions, however, are not usually melismatic. In fact, in *Mai finirò*, *Luci mie* and *Sento al cor* there are no melismas at all in the varied strophes; and in *V'è, v'è* there is but one extended melismatic passage in each strophe. Although the last two phrases of the second strophe of *Con voi* are melismatically elaborated, the melismas are short. In *La bella più bella* where there are also some florid divisions in the second strophe, they are limited to the penultimate phrase. The only virtuoso passage in these ostinato-variation cantatas occurs in the final statement of the first unit of *La bella più bella*, which is composed on the same basso ostinato as the second unit. Luigi recomposes the final phrases of the refrain and concludes the cantata with a long sequential melisma.

A general trait of the strophic variation cantata is that the recitative and arioso passages tend to be objects of variation considerably more consistently than other types of writing. One finds that in many of the cases where only one segment of a cantata undergoes variation in subsequent strophes, that segment is a recitative or an arioso. This is especially evident in the binary cantatas where the alternation of aria, recitative and/or arioso is more characteristic than it is in the other groups. The close alliance of word and music in a recitative or arioso makes it unfit for strophic repetition; hence the more frequent use of variation in this segment.

Among the strophic variations there is a particular group of cantatas, all binary, that incur somewhat more extensive variation than is generally typical.[115] These cantatas are distinguished by their exuberant melismatic passages—they can be appropriately termed virtuoso cantatas. In all ten cantatas, which are composed wholly or predominantly in duple meter, the most extensive variation usually occurs in the arioso segments in common-time (see *Quando spiega*, and *Precorrea*, exx. II, X). It is these segments that become elaborated into virtuoso melismatic passages.

Although Luigi tends to compose more elaborate settings for the second and third strophes of these cantatas, the process of embellishment is not necessarily a progressive one. The settings are dependent, as usual, on the texts. For example, the final phrase of the second strophe of *Hor ch'io vivo* is not melismatically ornamented as in the first strophe; besides the lack of embellishment, the variation here consists in the appearance of the minor subdominant of the subdominant. The eloquent use of D-flat, heard as part of the B-flat minor chord, expresses the *affetto* in the words "dolor vero" (ex. 71a). In other respects as well this cantata represents one of the more extreme examples of departure from the original; its three strophes are virtually three different settings. The variations are appropriate, for although the three strophes are poetically symmetrical, they contain no parallelisms and project different images. Evidence of the importance of the text in relationship to the music comes in the final strophe. Contrary to the usual procedure, it is the least embellished of the strophes. There are but three melismatic phrases and the last of these, the final passage, is one of the most concise and, at the same time, one of the most dramatic gestures of the cantata (ex. 71b). Luigi sets the text "E con rigor eterno sempre adduce al mio cor rigido il verno." The contractions, the terseness of most of the phrases, and the few *durezze* evoke the starkness and austerity suggested in the words.

In the cantata *Gelosia* Luigi uses another procedure. Here many of the passages in the three strophes are the same. It seems to me that this might be because the texts of the three strophes, unlike those of *Hor ch'io vivo*, all focus on one point—the hatefulness of jealousy. Variation occurs primarily in the opening passage and in the closing refrain—the latter an unusual feature since Luigi normally keeps the music of the refrain intact in the group of cantatas to which *Gelosia* belongs.

Internal Variation. As noted, the principle of strophic variation applies in only a fraction of Luigi's total cantata production. This should not obscure the fact that throughout that repertoire the principle of variation is applied internally in several ways. Its application is evident in the varying of recurring cadences and melody-types, in envelope settings, in varied openings of the recurrent ternary and rondo first units, and in other changes that occur in some of the recapitulations forming the ternary and rondo designs. Quoted material is usually altered in some way—by omissions, contractions, rhythmic shifts, slight melodic changes, and change of emphasis from one to another thematic motive.

A unique use of internal variation is found in the ternary cantata *Amor, e perche* (ex. XII). The bass of the second unit is formed of two slightly altered repetitions of the bass of the first unit, a rare relationship among the cantatas of two units of which I know no other example. The voice line of the second unit might be considered a variant of the first unit in its initial stages, but it soon departs from the original and is essentially through-composed. The procedure is that of the strophic bass—a bass line of several phrases is repeated with new melody and text.

Ostinato Procedures. Ostinato is not as prevalent as generally supposed. As far as I have determined, it is used relatively more often in the arie di più parti and laments than in the ariette corte; it occurs in 17 arie di più parti, three laments, nine binary cantatas, ten rondos, five rounded binary and two ternary cantatas.[116] Among all of these compositions there is but one in which ostinato is maintained from beginning to end.

The ostinato, then, is not primarily the carrier of entire large-scale structures, but a means of formal articulation and internal contrast. It is also a musical symbol of grief, despair, obstinacy or foolhardiness, and in a few ariette it sets an exclamatory verse apart from other verses. In keeping with the flexibility and the often segmentary character of the various designs, the ostinato is heard in one or another of the units, forming its whole or a segment of it—except, of course, for the rondo *La bella più bella*, the single cantata composed by Luigi on an ostinato bass from beginning to end.

The ostinato in nearly all ten rondo cantatas forms the whole of either one or the other of the two units, not merely a segment of a unit.[117] That the ostinato usually contrasts only the units themselves and not parts of either of them is probably due to the fact that segmentation of a unit is not characteristic of this group. In the binary cantatas, on the other hand, where segmentation is characteristic, the ostinato never forms the whole of a unit, but only a part of either one. In the six binary cantatas where ostinato occurs in the second unit, it embraces either the first or second of two segments—a setting of all but the concluding verse or couplet, or of the final verse alone. In *Deggio*, *E può* and *Ho perduto*, the ostinato forms the first part of the second unit and leads to the concluding segment. In *Tenti* and *De la vita*, two of the three cantatas that conclude with ostinato, the passage is a setting of the final verse; in *Dopo lungo penare* the ostinato is uniquely restricted to the cadential phrase. Of the three binary cantatas where the ostinato forms a segment of the first unit, *Ahi, dunque* and *Occhi belli, occhi miei* begin with an ostinato introduction, and *Guardate dove* contains the ostinato within the unit enframed by the introductory and concluding passages. The ostinato here is a setting of all but the identical first and last verses, and by contrast sets off the free passages of the envelope design.

Whereas metric segmentation is not a trait that the rounded binary cantatas share with the simple binary, the use of the ostinato in merely a segment of either of the two units is. In *Disperati* (ex. IV) and *Io non amo*, two of the three rounded binary cantatas where the ostinato occurs in the second unit, the ostinato is a setting of the first few verses, but not of all the verses preceding the final one. The ostinato passage is followed by a free segment, which in turn leads to the concluding passage. Thus the second units of these cantatas are like those of the binary cantatas that are formed of three distinct passages. In these two cantatas, as in the three binary pieces whose second units similarly begin with an ostinato, the ostinato separates the two units and reinforces a contrast already effected by metric change. In the third cantata in which the ostinato is a segment of the second unit, *M'uccidete*, the brief ostinato passage that begins after the first phrase does not segment the unit but apparently responds to the text. It is the setting of the unit's fourth verse alone, which, in the first strophe, refers to death's arrows fated to pierce the lover, and in the second, to the lover's miserable state. Nor does formal articulation seem to be the primary reason for the ostinato segments in the first units of *Rendetevi* and *Respira*. In the former the very brief ostinato follows the introductory passage and leads smoothly into the free passages that follow and conclude the unit; it is a lyrical, virtuoso setting of the exhortative couplet "Non contrastate più, libertà non si speri!" The beautiful cantata *Respira, core* (ex. V) begins with an ostinato that forms the introductory passage and continues up to the phrase that leads to the reprise of the opening verse. Here the ostinato has both structural and affective purposes.

The situation in *Fanciulle, tenete*, one of two ternary cantatas composed with ostinato, is the same as in the rondo cantatas. The contrast of ostinato with free bass marks the difference between the two units. In this cantata the ostinato also responds to a particular feature of the text—repetition reinforces the emphatic admonition of the single verse that forms the first unit: "Fanciulle, tenete il guard'a voi!". The ostinato, which sets the exclamation apart from the declarative verses that compose the rest of the text, moves in 6/8, a meter Luigi often uses for exhortative verses. A correlation between text and ostinato is also evident in the ternary cantata *Quando più mia libertà*, where, as in *M'uccidete*, the ostinato passage occurs within the second unit, setting off a single verse. The energetic coloratura passage on "il desir che le fa guerra!" emphasizes the word that is central to the posture of the text: "guerra" (ex. XXIII).

Not surprisingly, however, it is verses emphasizing immutability, obsession, constancy, perseverance, endurance, or firm resolution that are most commonly found with ostinato settings. In *Deggio dunque* the ostinato is joined to the assertion that love's remuneration is ever pain and more pain. In *E può soffrirsi* (ex. XV) the ostinato is introduced by the verse "E pur tant'ostinato adora le sue pene!" In *Guardate dove* the verses set with an ostinato bass—"segue tutta baldanza l'orme d'una beltà"—speak of a resolved but foolhardy lover who boldly tracks the footsteps of a beauty. Besides the ostinato bass repetition, the musical setting responds with constant eighth-note movement. Emphasized in the text of *Dopo lungo penare* is endurance. This is the unique cantata where ostinato occurs in the cadential phrase—the first strophe ends without repetition of the final cadence, but the second strophe closes with three statements of it and the third, with five. The increasing number of cadences is probably a musical joke inspired by the text, an impudent lover's challenge to Love: "Facciamo a chi può più!" In *Ho perduto* the lover advises his sorrowing thoughts to find Fortune and to pray her nevermore to leave them. "Pensieri dolenti" begins the second unit and with it the ostinato associated with grief—the descending chromatic tetrachord. Irony is clearly intended, for the final verse, the refrain of the cantata, set to a free bass, makes the humorous discovery: "Fortuna è dormite (*sic*)!"

The ostinato patterns are primarily variants of two prototypes: the descending Phrygian and major tetrachords (ex. 72). The one exception in all 26 ariette corte is the ostinato bass of *Luci mie* (ex. 73), which retains only the characteristic ending of the descending Phrygian tetrachord. Of the various extensions of the basic patterns, the most striking reappears in several rondos, but in none of Luigi's other cantatas containing an ostinato segment (exx. 74-77).

Usually an ostinato pattern is reiterated with rhythmic and even melodic alterations, a procedure consistent with Luigi's preference for asymmetry rather than symmetry in repetition (see exx. 78-82). In *La bella più bella*, for example, three variants of the primary ostinato pattern (ex. 83a) are freely interpolated within repetitions of it. The first variant (ex. 83b) is heard three times; the second (ex. 83c) once, and the third (ex. 83d) twice, but not in succession. In the ostinato bass of *Fanciulle, tenete* (ex. 84), only once does the basic pattern recur unembellished and unvaried—the other five statements are all slightly different. Although the free alteration of a basic pattern, such as the descending Phrygian tetrachord, with one of its variants, occurs quite frequently, the combination of two variants of a basic pattern in one long phrase, such as occurs in *Mai finirò* (ex. 75), is rare. Here Luigi forms an ostinato pattern combining the descending chromatic tetrachord[118] with the Phrygian variant also heard in *Con voi*, *Sento* and *V'è, v'è* (exx. 74, 76, 77). Another unusual procedure, one which in Luigi's cantatas occurs only in the last unit of *Su la veglia*, is a shift from one tonality and mode to another. The last unit begins with three statements of the descending major tetrachord C, B, A, G in C major—none of them the same; it then leads with a free transitional passage to the ostinato of the descending Phrygian tetrachord in the key of the relative minor (ex. 85).

Luigi adheres to no rigid manner of setting off, beginning or concluding an ostinato passage. For example, in *Tenti* and *De la vita*, the two binary cantatas in which the second unit concludes with an ostinato (in both the ostinato bass pattern is the descending D major tetrachord), the passage is prepared and concluded in entirely different ways. In *Tenti* the ostinato follows a modulation to the major dominant and begins after a cadence and with silence in the voice part for the first two beats. The ostinato design does not continue through the last measure, but is broken at the beginning of the last phrase, set to a free bass. Unlike the ostinato segment of *Tenti*, that of *De la vita* does not begin as a new and distinct passage, but begins as a melismatic extension of a cadence, the final tone of which becomes the first tone of the repeated bass tetrachord. Nor does the beginning of the ostinato coincide with the first statement of the final verse, as in *Tenti*, but begins with the conclusion of its first statement. And at the close of the cantata the ostinato is not broken for the final phrase, but continues to the very end.

The ostinato passages are usually composed in such a way that the vocal phrases do not constantly begin and end simultaneously with the ostinato pattern, but overlap the bass phrase or span two statements. Melismatic divisions, which regularly occur within an ostinato segment, avoid short phrases and frequent pauses. The florid movement frequently leads to a final phrase composed of a long sustained tone or of a reiterated tone.

Another kind of ostinato, primarily textual in conception but obviously not without its musical implications, is found in two of the ternary duos. As distinguished from simple text repetition, this kind of ostinato involves the reiteration of a few words in one voice during the singing of the rest of the text in the second voice. The repetition is not part of the original poetic structure, but is certainly a choice made by the composer for the purpose of emphasis. In *A te, mio core* the first verse is heard throughout the first unit. The introductory and concluding passages where both voices sing the verse several times comprise all but four of the 14 measures that compose the unit. In the four measures enframed by the envelope design the alto sings the remaining three verses while the soprano at four different times interjects the exclamation "a te!" With the last two syllables of the fourth verse sung by the alto, the soprano sings "mio cor!" Then together the two voices repeat the first verse until the final cadence. There is no muscial ostinato with this repetition, not even a rhythmic one, for the repeated words 'a te" occur with different rhythmic values.

Similarly in *Non mi lusingar* (ex. XXIV) the second verse "Non ti credo più no!" pervades most of the first unit after the introduction and all of the second unit up to the recapitulation of the first verse. In the first unit the alto continues to repeat the verse while the soprano sings the remaining verses; in the second unit, however, the voices exchange roles— the soprano repeats the exclamation while the alto sings the new text. In *Non mi lusingar*, unlike *A te*, some musical ostinato accompanies this text repetition. The eight statements of the verse—not counting the further sporadic repetition of the negative "no!"—are set with one rhythmic motive or a slight variant of it.[119]

The Melisma. Luigi's primary use of melisma in all four groups of ariette corte is to enhance and prolong the concluding passage of either or both units. Melismatic movement within the inner phrases of either unit occurs sporadically—a syllabic setting interspersed with two- or three-note groups is the norm. Within a musical unit, melisma prolongs a phrase, postpones a prepared cadence, disrupts a sequential pattern, and in ostinato passages provides contrast in the divisions over the repeated bass pattern: the melisma is always a factor of asymmetry.

Occasionally, too, melisma underscores a particular word and is a form of madrigalism. In the repertory of Luigi's cantatas, I have found that melismas heighten words that suggest movement: flight—"volate," "volo," "volando," "fugace"; the motion of the wind—"vento," "aura"; the movement of waves—"onda"; the state of inebriation—"liquor"; the agitated movement of conflict—"guerra," "sdegno"; the symbolic significance of resurrection—"risorgere"; the unfolding of a bird's wings—"dispiega," or of a ship's sails—"spiegò le vele," or figuratively, the opening of the voice in song, the motion of sounds—"sciolse il canto," "cantando"; words descriptive of vigorous or forceful motion—"precipitoso," "precipitarmi"; and words suggesting growth and increase—"cresce." Also in keeping with tradition, Luigi sets such words as "lieto," "contento," "gioia," and "ciel" with melisma. Although no actual motion is expressed in these words, figurative ascent is implied: the flight of the imagination, the fervor and exultation of the spirit.

Luigi constructs his melismas in a great many ways. Their direction and contour varies: some melismas begin and end on the same pitch and have a wavy contour, others are composed as a curve, some ascend to a climax then abruptly fall to a cadence, others begin in a high register and descend. The presence of sequence varies, as does its mode of employment: as we have seen, some melismas are composed almost entirely of sequences, others are only briefly sequential and still others are free of sequence; furthermore, the number of sequentially treated motives varies from one to several. Equally subject to variation is the kind of melodic movement employed: some melismas move entirely by step, others are characterized by broken triadic figures and other forms of disjunct motion. There is no usual melodic range: some melismas span only a third or fourth, others span the space of a sixth or seventh. In climactic passages the span is longer: a tenth or even an eleventh. Rhythmic figures vary from even-note runs to dotted-note patterns and mixed configurations. The accompanying basso continuo may be of several types: one kind of melisma is constructed on a pedal bass, another on slow moving measured notes, another on an active bass that moves in contrary motion; and still another is composed with a parallel bass that reinforces the initial tones of the various melodic segments at the tenth below. Certainly the brevity or the length of the melisma is a factor in determining its various aspects. And surely the text is influential in determining both the length and the shape of a melisma. A melisma with the word "costante" is quite different from one with "volante."

There are, however, general characteristics. The melodic and rhythmic motives of a melismatic passage are not normally culled from the body of the cantata, but are stock gruppetti, scale passages, chordal ascents and descents, written-out trill repetitions. Characteristic in melismas composed of scale runs is a large connecting skip between two of them (exx. 86-88). Similarly, in those melismas in which there is a gradual ascent to the climactic tone, the latter is often succeeded by a diminished seventh, an octave, or an even larger downward leap, with a brief cadential gesture in the lower register concluding the phrase (ex. II, second strophe; ex. 89). Disjunct movement of all kinds is, of course, governed by the prevailing harmony, though there are numerous instances of rapid changing-tones and auxiliaries approached by leap (see the second-strophe variant of measure 28 in ex. II), occasionally resulting in momentary cross-relations (ex. 90). An embellished melodic pedal tone is consistently formed of circular reiterated gruppetti and trill-like alternations—a kind of figuration that creates an illusion of mobility (exx. 91-93). In the cantatas where it occurs such embellishment usually ornaments an important cadential point.

Longer melismas are generally motivically uniform, or nearly so— the selection of cantatas provides numerous illustrations of this. But there are also many instances of long melismas like that in the aria di più parti *E che cantar* (ex. 88), with its combination of scale passages, gruppetti and accenti, that typify Luigi's overall avoidance of uniformity in both rhythmic and melodic respects. One finds such melismas occasionally in the ariette corte (see ex. X), but they more often appear in the arie di più parti.

Almost by definition in Luigi's style, a melisma is the carrier of accent. Accordingly, its placement is usually on the penultimate or final syllable of a word.[120] In the rare instances when a melisma is placed on a monosyllable, the monosyllable is an accented one; it is almost never a preposition, conjunction, or article. Melismas are usually sung on the vowels, a, e and o; infrequently on the vowels i and u.

Melismas for two voices are often composed in parallel thirds and sixths (exx. 94, 95), or with the separate voices imitating each other in turn (ex. 90); the two procedures are also combined. In a modification of the second procedure, the manner of composition is reminiscent of the contemporary keyboard style: each voice carries its configurations in turn; while one voice sustains a tone, the other voice takes up the melismatic movement and then there is an exchange of roles. The final chord at the end of the passage sometimes emerges from a "frenzy of movement"[121] (ex. 96). But rhapsodic melismatic passages for more than one voice are rare. Another device that Luigi uses only occasionally is the combination of syllabic or nearly syllabic movement in the one voice with melismatic extension in the second (ex. 97).

We know little about the manner in which melismatic passages were performed. No doubt they were sung with special affective nuances. An indication of this is a rare rubric in the MS *I* Rvat, Barb. 4204, f. 155v that requires a melismatic passage to be performed "ondeggiato, piano e forte" (ex. 98).

Evidence in the MS sources also points to the possibility that melismatic passages were variable events in the cantatas. The most frequent divergences among different sources of the same work occur in the melismatic passages—these are in most instances the only substantial variants.[122] What is varied is usually only the embellishment itself and frequently also its length, but not the harmony or the underlying melodic shape of the passage. The reasons for such discrepancies among the sources are difficult to identify precisely. It is possible that two versions are preserved: an early one and a later reworking. It is also conceivable that the copyists attempted to approximate in their notation the melismas and variations improvised by the singers. Still another possibility is that the composer made changes to suit the singers by whom the cantatas were to be performed. A cantata that points to this possibility is *Chiuda quest'occhi*. The MS *I* Rvat, 4374, which preserves a more simple melodic line than that found in the other two sources, notates the cantata for tenor voice; the embellished version is notated for soprano. This, to be sure, is inadequate evidence—it can also be used to support either of the other suggested reasons. The question remains open and deserves investigation.

Chapter 3

Ariette Corte: The Individual Formal Designs

As a supplement to the preceding discussion, which has attempted to characterize the repertory of ariette corte as a whole, it may be useful to deal individually with the principal formal types, briefly recalling and further illustrating their distinguishing traits, and pointing out some of their exceptional manifestations.

The Binary Form

The most common musical form in the cantatas of Luigi Rossi is the binary design. The two groups treated here are the simple binary cantatas of one or more strophes without refrain, of which there are 79, and the strophic pieces with closing refrain, of which there are 42. The 19 rounded binary cantatas will be dealt with separately because of their special features.

We tend to think of the binary form of the Baroque in terms of instrumental music, in terms of the dances of the suites where a reigning characteristic is consistency in the material used. But the binary design of the mid-century cantata couples a set of recognizable formal conventions with a supple response to a text frequently designed to produce a variety of contrasts. The result is an extreme flexibility at the local formal level, dictated less often by outward details of versification than by considerations of text expressivity. In the binary arietta—by no means a lightweight ditty of little significane, but "arietta" simply by comparison to the multi-movement aria di più parti—this expressivity is principally accomplished on the formal level through techniques of segmentation.

As will be recalled, the two major units of the binary cantata are distinct and separate. The tonal goal of each is the same; in a small number of cantatas the cadences are nearly identical. Prolongation and melismatic cadences are used at the close of both units, but ritornelli occur infrequently. Internal cadences to the secondary degrees, primarily the dominant and the relative major or minor, are usual in both units, but more numerous and generally wider-ranging in the second than in the first.

The first unit generally begins with a motto or with a longer introductory passage; only rarely does this return at the close of the unit, forming what I have called an envelope design. Except for the articulation of the opening, the first unit is rarely segmented. It is usually shorter than the second and contrasts with it in some way.

Metric change, modulation away from the tonic, the skip of an octave or tenth, staggered entries—these mark the beginning of the second unit. Often the contrast is thematic. A trait of the second unit is segmentation. The conclusion, usually a movement in triple meter, makes up most of the unit, although it is generally the setting of no more than a single verse, usually a hendecasyllable. A recitative passage often leads to the concluding segment, pausing on the dominant or another secondary degree, but rarely on the tonic.

Peculiar Traits. This summary reminds us that the flexible, segmentary quality of Luigi's binary design derives in large part from his frequent use of metric and stylistic and tempo changes, but that these are generally confined to the second unit, setting off the concluding segment, and/or the passage preceding it, especially when this is a recitative. Next in order of frequency is change from one unit to the next. Metric or other stylistic contrast within the first unit occurs least of all; here it sets off the introductory gesture or the concluding segment, or is a means of emphasizing a particular word or verse. It would appear, then, that a formal convention is at work; one that may on occasion give way to considerations of expression, syntax, and emphasis, but that frequently overrides any consideration of poetic meter. For example, in *Ha cent'occhi* a change to triple meter is made in the second unit despite the fact that the poetic meter remains stable—the verses are all octosyllables. The shift is apparently governed solely by the convention of setting off the concluding passage from the rest of the unit. In *O cieli*, on the other hand, the entire first unit is in 6/4 despite the fact that the poetic meter fluctuates—impari verses follow the opening hexasyllables. This is in keeping with the general practice of retaining a single meter throughout the first unit.

A further illustration of the apparent subjugation of verse-metrical to musical-metrical design considerations can be seen in connection with Luigi's use of recitative. As was pointed out earlier, recitative is usually found in conjunction with impari verses. In *Un tiranno*, however, we find a rare example of it as a setting of octosyllables. The apparent reason for this is the occurrence of the octosyllables between the first unit and the concluding verse of the second, a point in the formal design that requires a transition between two movements in aria. Recitative is Luigi's most usual means of achieving this, and the use of recitative in the binary cantatas is more frequent, and more consistent as to placement, than among the remaining ariette corte. It usually forms the whole of the opening segment of the second unit leading to the conclusion, or it is the central passage of the second unit leading from the first period, which has continued the movement of the preceding unit, or has changed to another meter, to the longer conclusion. Unlike later Baroque vocal music, in these cantatas the recitative passage is not separated from the aria movements, but merges smoothly with them.

A further distinguishing trait of the binary cantatas is the extent of the setting of the final words of the second unit. The music for the final verse and its repetitions usually makes up most of this unit.[1] As one might expect, the use of sequence is comparatively frequent in such passages. A few cantatas, particularly ensembles, go beyond sequential or other simple repetition to a more elaborate working out of one or more central motives from the initial statement of the final verse. This can be seen in *Pietà, spietati lumi* (ex. XXI) or in *Si o no*, each of whose phrases preceding the final cadential phrase begins with the same motive.[2]

Notwithstanding the occasionally ostinato-like effect of such passages, ostinato itself is rare. When used, it sets off one or another of the units; never does it pervade the whole cantata. Nor is strophic variation prevalent, either in terms of the number of cantatas employing it (23 of the total 121 simple binary pieces), or in terms of its amount and extent within the individual piece. As was pointed out in Chapter 2, varied strophes rarely present substantial or extensive differences from the first setting. Usually the changes occur sporadically within the strophe, interspersed with wholly unaltered passages. Variation consists both of purely melodic embellishment and of rhythmic and thematic changes that better suit the new text. The infrequent harmonic changes are principally the result of rhythmic displacements, of augmentation and diminution of the time values.

The practice of relating the concluding passages of the two units of the binary design by recurring cadences recalls the distinguishing trait of the rounded binary design—the identity or near-identity of the closing segments of the two units. Though not extensive, this practice is more characteristic of the binary cantatas than it is of the ternary and rondo groups.[3] The recurring cadence with new text is generally composed at the same pitch level and in the same meter, though there are examples of both transposition and metric change. The cadences are never exactly alike, however. Alteration of some kind—melodic, rhythmic, harmonic, or exchange of vocal lines in the ensembles—results in variation. The reason for the alterations in some cases is clearly textual, as in the closing binary arietta of the aria di più parti *Ferma, Giove* (ex. 99).[4] Beyond this, of course, differences also result from the fact that each cadence is an integral part of its own unit and is the consequence of what precedes it.

A Representative Binary Cantata. Since *Gelosia* has been singled out by Parry and Prunières as an example of the attention Rossi gave to the matter of form, as an example of music which speaks both for itself and for the enhancement of the text,[5] I should like to add a few more specific remarks about this cantata. Although both historians convey an appreciation of its structural organization, neither discusses *Gelosia*'s exemplary binary design nor the significance of its features.[6]

Unless one realizes Luigi's predilection for opening mottoes, the meaning of the first measure of each of the three strophes is lost. The terse setting of the first three syllables announces the cantata; in performance, a pause should separate it from the first full phrase. The degree of melodic activity following the brief introductory gesture is unusual— Luigi's cantatas rarely begin with extended melismatic passages—but the setting responds to the text: "Gelosia che poco a poco nel mio cor serpendo vai." It conveys the insinuating activity of jealousy. A confirmation of this is the simplification of the passage in the third strophe, where no strong metaphor appears. The movement from tonic to dominant in this opening passage and the pause on the Phrygian cadence at its close are typical. A marked contrast in style separates this from the second segment of the first unit. Luigi sets the second pair of octosyllable verses in aria in common-time. This segment of the cantata is hardly varied at all, in keeping with a general tendency to alter least where movement in aria is involved. The second unit begins with a change to a lyric 6/4 passage fitting a couplet of impari verses. The contrast of the two units is of course characteristic of the binary design. The next passage is the usual recitative that leads to the refrain conclusion. Duple meter in the setting of the refrain verse, however, is unusual—triple meter is typical. But the duple meter is purposely chosen for the rhapsodic setting fitting the exclamation "Lasciami, Gelosia!"

In the second unit the opening passage is varied only in the second strophe in order to fit the word "dimmi" that replaces "da me" of both the first and third strophes. The short recitative, too, is left untouched except in the second strophe where a change responds to the word "ohime." The most extensive variations occur in the concluding segment, the refrain.[7] Of the closing melismas, that of the second strophe is the

most involved and virtuosic passage. But in the MS SF de Bellis, Misc.
V. LXIX the closing passages of the second and third strophes are not the
same as those given in the other sources; in this version the refrain becomes progressively more elaborate. This version also avoids the unusual
cadence at the end of the cantata, a cadence that occurs only in *Gelosia*
among the ariette corte (ex. 100a). A few other cantatas end with the fifth
of the final chord in the vocal line; it is the leading tone to the dominant
immediately preceding that is unique. The de Bellis source preserves a
more conventional conclusion—it ends with the most elaborate setting of
the refrain verse and with a perfect cadence to the tonic (ex. 100b).

Unusual Realizations of the Binary Design. Wherever more than one
stanza of poetry is involved, the binary cantatas are either strophically
repeated or strophically varied along the lines described in the previous
chapter. However, a binary piece contained within the aria di più parti *O
dura* is composed in another manner. The second stanza of the symmetrical strophic binary text is set in part to the original music and in
part to new music. The first unit is composed in the usual manner: the
original setting is retained for the new quatrain. But the first unit of the
second strophe is not separated from the second unit as it was in the
original setting; it is elided with a new setting of the verses of the second
unit preceding the closing refrain. This segment of the second unit, newly-
composed and appended to the first unit, leads to the recapitulation of
the original conclusion with the refrain text. Carissimi, who also set the
text, composes the symmetric strophes in another way. He sets anew all
but the closing refrain of the second strophe, another unusual procedure.
Unconventional, too, is Carissimi's avoidance of the primary tonality at
the close of the first unit in both strophes.

   Non m'affligete, a binary cantata with some unusual features
(ex. XXV), is attributed to Luigi in the posthumous Pignani publication
of 1679 and is not found anywhere else. I question whether the cantata
is Luigi's. Several outstanding musical traits of the cantata are not at all
characteristic of Luigi's style. The manner of executing the envelope design of the first unit is not typical of Luigi, who rarely quotes the opening
passage intact at the close of the first unit. Nor are the frequent recurrences of entire musical phrases with new text both within a unit and
from one unit to the next to be found in any of Luigi's ariette corte.[8]
There is more repetition in *Non m'affligete* than one normally hears in
any of his cantatas. Another factor that tends to belie Luigi's authorship
is the recurrence of the chord of the lowered second degree. Luigi uses
this chord much more sparingly; in fact, one rarely finds it at all except
in a final cadence. Furthermore, when the lowered second degree is used

in a cadence it is mostly realized without the diminished third in the melodic line. As far as I have determined, the affective interval appears in only three of Luigi's cantatas (excluding *Non m'affligete*), and in all three it is heard but once, in the concluding passage.[9] I should not be surprised if a manuscript is found with this cantata attributed to a composer of the generation following Luigi's.

The Rondo Form

Fifty-four ariette corte are rondos and four arie di più parti have the overall design of the rondo form,[10] while six other arie di più parti contain a rondo within them.[11] There are three kinds of rondo designs: the strophic rondo, of which there are 33 single ariette and one contained within the aria di più parti *Da perfida*; the rondo with strophic variations, of which there are 12 single ariette and three contained within *Giusto così*, *Sopra conca* and *V'è, v'è*; and the rondo of three or more units, of which there are nine ariette, two contained within *Ombre fuggite* and *S'era alquanto*, and the four arie di più parti having an overall rondo design.

The strophic and the strophically varied rondos usually have but two recurrences of the first unit-refrain and one recurrence of the second unit (A b A b A). Only five cantatas have a second additional stanza for the second unit requiring one more recurrence of each unit (A b A b A b A),[12] and only *Fanciulla son'io* has four stanzas of text for the second unit thus requiring two additional recurrences of both units.

Instead of a strophic repetition of the second unit, the rondo of three or more units has different musical settings for the verses that occur between statements of the refrain. Most of the rondos of this type have but one unit between two statements of the refrain: A b A c A. The four arie di più parti whose overall design is the rondo form, however, contain additional units between appearances of the refrain; each of these cantatas has its own design. *Non più viltà*, for example, has the form AB c d B e f B g AB (A and B represent the two segments of the refrain; c, e and g are units composed in recitative, and d and f, units set as arias in triple meter). Except for the rondo frame, the design of *Ferma, Giove* is quite different: A b C C A dEf d'Ef'A. The refrain (A) is a miniature ternary piece, b is an aria in triple meter concluded by a phrase of recitative, C is a phrase of recitative followed by an aria in common-time, the whole of which is repeated, text and music; dEf are, respectively, a recitative, an aria passage introduced by a short phrase of recitative and a concluding recitative; d'Ef' is the strophic repetition of dEf with the second segment, the aria and its introductory recitative passage, recurring with the same words. Since these four extended rondos are properly arie di più parti, they will be largely excluded from the remarks that follow, which deal with the 54 cantatas whose rondo design is unmixed with other structural patterns.

The Basic Design. There are few internal formal earmarks that are peculiar to the rondo cantatas alone; most of the traits of this group are shared by the ternary cantatas. The two basic musical units of both types are, like those of the binary and rounded binary, distinct and separate, but because the second unit leads immediately to the recapitulation of the first without pause, it does not usually have the complete and formal close that is characteristic of the binary and rounded binary second units. This merging of the second unit with the recapitulation of the first also accounts for several other traits that distinguish the ternary and rondo groups from the binary and rounded binary: the conclusion of the second unit in some of the cantatas in a related key rather than in the primary tonality; the absence of ritornello and the relative infrequency of prolongation at the close of the second unit; and the rarity of identical or nearly-identical cadences at the close of both units.

Except for the articulation that results from the envelope design, which occurs more frequently in the ternary and rondo cantatas than in the binary, but less frequently than in the rounded binary, the first unit is seldom segmented. It is generally somewhat shorter in length than the second unit and its tonal range is more concentrated, often limited to the primary tonality and one or two related keys. Like the binary and rounded binary first units, those of the ternary and rondo cantatas conclude with extended cadential passages marked by one or more of the devices of prolongation: postponement of the dominant's resolution, melismatic extension, or repetition. Sequential techniques, usually involving text repetition, are common in the closing phrases of the first unit. Although it is by no means frequent in the sources, a ritornello reaffirming the final cadence of the first unit is more characteristic of the ternary and rondo cantatas than of the binary and rounded binary.

Metric, stylistic, or tempo changes in both ternary and rondo cantatas usually come at the outset of the second unit, thereby distinctly separating the two units. Metric change within the second unit is less common than in the binary cantatas. When segmentation does occur, the division of the second unit is not like that of the binary and rounded binary designs. Since the final verse of the ternary and rondo second units is not normally a recurring refrain verse, nor a reprise quoted from the first unit, nor a gnomic statement summarizing the gist of the cantata, it is not usually set apart from the rest. If the second unit is segmented at all, its articulation is such that the text's two quatrains (or similar equal or nearly-equal groups of verses) are separated. This two-part division will be further discussed below.

The second unit, like that of the other formal types, is usually marked by increased harmonic activity in the form of modulations to related keys not touched upon in the first unit, by a tendency to avoid the primary tonality in moving constantly from one to another of the closely related keys, and by a more frequent use of the sequence of descending or ascending fifths within one or more phrases. However, because text repetition is not a general trait of the ternary and rondo second units, sequence is not as common here as in the binary and rounded binary second units.

Although it is not a distinguishing trait, ostinato is relatively more frequent in the ternary and rondo cantatas than in the other two groups. But it does not usually form a segment of a unit as in the binary and rounded binary cantatas; instead, ostinato passages tend to encompass the whole of one or the other unit, thereby unifying rather than segmenting it internally. As was observed in Chapter 2, strophic variation is not common in the group under discussion. Lacking altogether in the ternary cantatas, it is limited in the rondos to those cantatas with an ostinato bass. As in the strophically varied binary and rounded binary cantatas, the variations never radically alter the original setting.

What primarily distinguishes the ternary and rondo cantatas are their different patterns of strophic repetition. Whereas the three-part design is strophically repeated as a whole, each unit with new text, the rondo five- or seven- or nine-part design is not. Here only the second unit is assigned a new poetic strophe; the first unit follows it each time with its original text. In the ternary design the first unit never alternates with the second in this manner, but always enframes it.

Another distinction between the two groups is the different manner of treating the recapitulation of the first unit. In the ternary cantatas the recapitulated first unit is rarely altered; in the rondos, on the other hand, it is rather frequently varied or extended as in strophic variations, occasionally with some extensive changes in particular phrases. In other cases it may be shortened in its "internal" reappearances—i.e. those prior to its final restatement at the close of the cantata. The several types of varied reprise will be explored in detail below.

Peculiar Traits. As noted in the preceding summary, both the rondo and ternary cantatas proceed rather differently from the other groups with regard to segmentation of their second units. Frequently they display no marked internal division of the unit, but where a formal articulation is found (in about one fourth of the cantatas of both groups),[13] it corresponds to a division of the text into equal or nearly-equal halves, usually two quatrains, in place of the setting-off of a single final verse seen in the binary cantatas. The two-part design is articulated by a caesura on the dominant or tonic at the close of the first quatrain. It is is usually marked by double bars, and displays one of the following features: a ritornello at the conclusion of the first part, a metric shift or a change from aria movement in common-time to recitative, the contrast of an ostinato with a free bass, or a pause in the vocal line with the continuo initiating the second section. In several of these two-part units the second section is initiated with a strong opening gesture. Full-fledged binary designs are exceptional. Only in the rondos *Hor guardate* and *Si v'ingannate* and the ternary *Non c'è che dire* are the two parts of the second unit distinguished by the typical features of the binary form. For example, in *Si v'ingannate* both parts close with perfect cadences to the tonic; metric change marks the opening of the second part and also sets off the concluding segment, and, as so often happens in the binary cantatas, the concluding passage is preceded by a cadence to the dominant, here a Phrygian cadence. Although the recitative quality of the conclusion is unusual—most binary pieces close in triple meter—the double cadences that form its final phrase are typical of full-fledged binary strophes.

A unique version of the binary design is the second unit of *Hor guardate* (ex. IX). The first part begins and concludes in C major, the tonality of the cantata. The second part modulates immediately to the relative minor; its first goal is a Phrygian cadence to the dominant of that key (m. 35). The concluding segment follows a perfect cadence to the relative minor and contrasts in style with the rest of the section. All this is quite regular. The extraordinary features begin with this concluding passage: it recapitulates the opening verse of the refrain and is a variant of the original setting (this also happens in the rondo *Speranze, che dite*). Although the relationship of the close of the second unit to the opening of the refrain is quite unusual, a still more extraordinary event follows. The ritornello that reaffirms the cadence of the reprise-conclusion leads to the recapitulation of the entire second section of the second unit up to the concluding segment. At this point the refrain returns. It seems to me that Luigi interpolates this segment in order to avoid the successive repetition of the opening verse.

The second, third and other additional units of the nonstrophic rondos are composed like the second unit of the strophic form—they contrast metrically, stylistically, and thematically with the first unit; and in the few cases where segmentation occurs, they are usually articulated into two nearly equal halves. The various units that alternate with the recurring refrain can differ completely from one another; or they can be related by migrating phrases, by similar thematic material, by recurrent structural designs, and by a common tonal scheme. The degree of relationship seems to depend in part upon the text. In *Speranze, sentite*, for example, the symmetry of the texts of the second and third units—they are stanzas alike in number of verses, rhyme scheme and verse lengths—is reflected in the close correspondence between their musical settings. The third unit (see ex. XIII) retains the meter and the basic harmonic goals of the second unit, begins with the same four measures and quotes the eight measures of its third phrase from the second half of the preceding unit—measures 36 through 44 of the second unit are measures 19 through 27 of the third. The tonal goal that precedes the quoted phrase is also the same. Further relationships are the Phrygian cadence to the dominant with which the two units begin, the ascending fourth initiating the second half of each of the two units, and the cadential goals G major, A minor and B (the relative major, the subdominant and the dominant), which occur, however, in different order.[14]

Unlike the inner units of *Speranze, sentite*, those of *Mi contento* contrast. The differences among the units reflect the various poetic designs of their texts. The octosyllables of the second unit are set in aria in common-time except for the last couplet, which functions as transition to the refrain and is set in recitative. The hexasyllables of the third unit are set throughout in 6/8. The fourth unit, unlike the previous unsegmented one, is a binary arietta. The first part is an aria setting of octosyllables in common-time; the second, a setting of hexasyllables in 3/4. The primary thematic motives of each section are migrating motives associated respectively with octosyllables and hexasyllables (the "Adorate" and "Sperate" motives). Also noteworthy is the fact that this miniature binary unit is the only one of the three that begins with a motto introduction and closes with an exact repetition of the final cadence—both being features of the binary design.

The recitative-aria pair, consisting of a movement in aria preceded by a substantial passage (as opposed to a brief introductory or transitional phrase) of recitative, is not characteristic of the strophic rondos or of the ariette corte in general, but is a feature of three arie di più parti that contain a rondo unit or have its overall design. Although there are very few cantatas whose approximate date of composition we know, it seems to me that these arie di più parti—*Ombre, fuggite, Se non corre* and *Non più viltà*—are among Luigi's late works and that the recitative-aria pair is a design that occurs primarily in Luigi's late cantatas.

As noted earlier, another trait peculiar to the rondo design is the practice of varying, extending, curtailing or otherwise altering the setting of the first unit-refrain in its various recapitulations. In the ternary cantatas the recapitulation of the first unit is usually exact, without change except for a slight variation or adjustment in the opening phrase in two cantatas (*Il contento* and *Su, su, begl'occhi*). Interestingly, the only ternary cantata in which there is considerable difference in the second statement of the reprise is *Cor dolente*, which in one source appears as a rondo.[15] On the other hand, about one fourth of the rondo first units undergo alteration in their recapitulation.[16] The change in some of the cantatas is merely the substitution of a new opening phrase; more frequently it involves melodic variations, slight extensions, or a new version of the closing phrase. Radical differences, transforming the second and third statements of the refrain almost into new settings, are exceptional: they occur only in the arie di più parti *Se mi volete* and *S'era alquanto*. In the cantatas where change entails both musical and textual curtailment the curtailed version is usually the second refrain statement and not the last.[17] The text is a single verse or couplet of the original text and its setting is either quoted from the original setting or newly-composed. The curtailed refrain is neither an independent unit, nor the conclusion of the second unit; it is a bridge between the second unit and its strophic repetition.

Changes that occur in the beginning of the refrain normally effect a smoother transition from the close of the second unit, often by emphatically reaffirming the return to the tonic after the modulation at the close of the second unit. Other changes produce a varied and asymmetrical realization of the basic design.

The alterations in the recapitulation of the first unit of *Quanto è credulo* (ex. XXVI) merit attention, for they exemplify the means Luigi uses in contrasting the related settings and in achieving a developed musical form.[18] The primary changes are made in the setting of the first (and last) verse. In its first appearance the refrain conclusion (first ending) quotes the last two- and-one-half measures of the introduction, but briefly prefaces them with a new setting of the opening words that announces the thematic motives of the quoted segment. The economy of thematic material is such that this new beginning is a variant of the cantata's opening measure. There is no envelope design in the second refrain statement since the refrain here is curtailed to one verse: "Quanto è credulo il mio core!"—the first (and last) verse of the whole refrain text. This setting of the reprise verse (second ending) begins with the opening measure of the cantata, then continues with a variant of the second and third measures, an extension of the third measure and a new conclusion. The third statement of the refrain returns to the original complete setting, which it recapitulates in part. The changes include a measure of melisma inserted between the seventh and eighth measures, then, beginning with the third beat of the original ninth measure, a new setting of the fourth verse, "Ne d'inganni ha poi timore," which leads to the conclusion. The conclusion (third ending), the fourth appearance of the reprise verse, begins like the conclusion of the first statement of the refrain, but then quotes and extends the curtailed second refrain statement and concludes with a new cadential phrase. It is interesting that with each successive statement of the refrain Luigi increases the number of cadential phrases to the tonic— the first refrain concludes with a single one, the second is formed of two, and the conclusion of the third is composed of three cadential phrases.

Another kind of curtailment occurs in the duo *Tu sarai*, whose refrain is a ternary design:

A.   Tu sarai sempre il mio bene
       la mia vita, il cor mio.

3/2, 14 measures beginning and ending in C minor,

B.   Ne perch'io viva in pene
       cangerò mai desio.

3/2, 13 measures also beginning and ending in C minor,

A.   recapitulated intact.

Following the second unit and its strophic repetitions, the refrain is recapitulated beginning with the second couplet: ABA c BA c BA. This arrangement, particularly in view of the relative brevity of the second unit as compared to the refrain, gives *Tu sarai* an overall structure not unlike that of certain strophic rounded binary cantatas: ABA cBA cBA. There is, however, a significant difference in that the recapitulation of all the verses of the first unit at the close of the second is a procedure characteristic of the rondo, but not of the rounded binary design. *Tu sarai*, then, is best classified as a rondo, albeit a somewhat exceptional one.

Still another kind of curtailment is the omission of the introductory passage, a peculiar trait of four rondo cantatas (*Ch'io speri*, *Con voi parlo*, *Deh, soffri* and *Speranze, che dite*). What this omission implies, it seems to me, is the dispensable quality of the cantata's opening phrase when its function is primarily and distinctly introductory and when it is separated from the body of the first unit. In all four cantatas the phrase is a brief but strong assertion of the primary tonality that comes to a close with a cadence on the tonic. After a silence the second phrase begins with renewed impetus on an upbeat, in two of the cantatas with a change of meter. The opening words omitted with the introductory phrase in *Deh, soffri* and *Ch'io speri* are respectively an exhortation and a rhetorical question whose curtailment does not alter the meaning of the refrain nor lessen its impact. In *Con voi* the first verse is retained in the body of the refrain—its repetition forms the first phrase of the refrain proper. In *Speranze, che dite*, the independent exclamation is used at the close of each unit. The phrase that follows the introductory gesture fits the conclusion of the second unit and forms a good beginning to the refrain except in *Ch'io speri*. In this cantata the new first phrase is altered so that it makes an effective beginning.

The omission is not immediately evident in *Speranze, che dite* (ex. XXVII), for although the first couplet does not return at the beginning of the subsequent statements of the refrain, it is recapitulated at the close of each of the inner units.[19] Luigi recomposes the couplet as if it were part of an envelope design, or the reprise of a rounded binary form. The new and longer setting is clearly derived from the original phrase; Luigi quotes its opening in the key of the relative minor. In the third unit the sarabande-like rhythmic motive of the opening pervades the whole of the last segment; in a phrase constructed on an ascending chromatic bass, it is heard at the head of a design repeated sequentially. Unless the function of the second, longer setting of the couplet as a closing period is understood, it will be mistaken as the new opening of the refrain. But this properly begins with the change to 3/8 and the verse "Andate che siete."

One wonders if this kind of curtailment was more common than the sources indicate, and if the opening phrase of other rondo refrains were similarly intended only for the very beginning of the cantata.[20] Certainly in the four cantatas where it is notated the abbreviation is satisfactory both textually and musically. An obvious starting-point for future investigation of the problem would be to determine what proportion of the rondo repertory might lend itself equally well to the same procedure.

The Ternary Form

Only a small number—22—of the cantatas are ternary.[21] The first unit, text and music, begins and concludes the cantata enframing the second unit. In the strophic form (six of the 22 cantatas are strophic) the whole three-part design is repeated with new text. With prime (') representing new text, the strophic form is A b A // A' b' A' //.

The two units correspond exactly to the two units of the strophic rondo. If the ternary cantata were given an additional text for the second unit alone, and its first unit recapitulated again after the strophic repetition of the second unit, the result would be a rondo. Several rondos, in fact, appear as ternary pieces in some sources because of the omission of text for the strophic repetition of the second unit. *Cor dolente*, one of these, is included among the ternary pieces because its notation as a ternary cantata is not merely the result of the omission of the second strophe, but represents a more developed musical version (see above, p. 99). Since the features that distinguish the rondo form from the ternary, and the basic traits that these two designs have in common, are discussed and summarized in the previous chapter, my remarks here will concern some variants of the basic design and unusual traits of particular ternary cantatas.

Variants of the usual reprise scheme occur in *Tu parti, core* and *Fanciulle, tenete*. Although the texts of both have typical designs—quatrains followed by second units of eight and five verses, respectively—in both the original reprise quatrain is curtailed. It is segmented musically in such a way that only the first verse serves as reprise and the other three verses are incorporated into the second unit. In *Tu parti* a cadence to the tonic and a double bar with repeat dots set off the first verse. The next three verses lead as introductory phrases to the main part of the second unit, which begins with a change of tempo (the notation changes from 6/2 to 6/4). Similarly in *Fanciulle, tenete* a double cadence to the tonic and a double bar emphatically set the first verse apart as reprise. The rest of the opening quatrain is not set off from the second unit by a change of meter, as in *Tu parti*, but it is nonetheless clearly articulated by the recurrence of the ritornello conclusion of the reprise verse. Verses 2-4 make up the first half of the second unit.

1st unit-reprise:

        Tu parti, core, addio!

2nd unit:

        Va dove vuoi tu,
        non ti comando più
        perche più non sei mio.

        Va in quel seno
        ch'amore t'addita,
        ma v'entra almeno
        per la ferita
        ch'egli v'aprì.
        Si, altrimenti
        vivrem dolenti
        e tu ed io.

reprise:

        Tu parti, core, addio!

1st unit-reprise:

        Fanciulle, tenete il guardo a voi!

2nd unit:

        C'ha giurato un sol Zerbino
        farvi tutto ad uno inchino
        spasimar e crepar de' fatti suoi.

        Eccolo che sen viene
        tutto fe, tutto spene,
        a farvi guerra.
        Chinate gl'occhi a terra,
        e no'l mirate mai prima ne poi.

reprise:

        Fanciulle, tenete il guardo a voi!

Only *Disperate speranze* among the rest of the ternary cantatas has a first unit consisting of a single verse. The text of this cantata, the shortest of the ternary texts, is made up of a single stanza. The first and last of the six verses are identical—a reprise of one verse; the four inner verses from the second unit.

The text of the ternary cantata *Non mi lusingar* deserves special mention because it is the only one known to be derived from a longer and more complex cantata. The text is based on the first 12 verses of a cantata by Marc'Antonio Pasqualini:

        Non mi lusingar più, speranza infida!
        Non ti credo più, no!
        Colei che mi ferì
        d'amarmi si pentì;
        ad altro amante l'amor mio donò.
        Lascia, dunque, ch'il duolo, homai, m'uccida!
        Ho scoperto gl'inganni,
        speme rea, ch'io ti creda mai più invan t'affanni.
        Nel mio crudel martire,
        si che voglio morire!
        Da i colpi della sorte
        non puo liberar altri che morte.[22]

The first unit consists of the first five verses of Pasqualini's cantata, followed by a new sixth verse that rhymes with the first, and concluding with a return of the first verse itself. The second unit is a rearrangement of the sixth, seventh, eighth, eleventh and twelfth verses of the original text. The sixth is taken as the last of the five verses since it rhymes with the opening verse, which once again returns as conclusion—a unique

instance in the ternary cantatas. The cantata closes with a recapitulation
of the rest of the first unit, the second through the seventh verses (the
first verse returns as the seventh).

1st unit-reprise:

> Non mi lusingar più, speranza infida!
>
> Non ti credo più, no!
> Colei che mi ferì
> d'amarmi si pentì;
> ad altro amante l'amor mio donò,
> e del mio fido cor fui l'omicida.
> Non mi lusingar più, speranza infida!

2nd unit:

> Ho scoperto gl'inganni,
> speme rea, ch'io ti creda invan t'affani.
> Da i colpi della sorte
> Non puo liberar altro che morte.
> Lascia, dunque, ch'il duol homai m'uccida!
> Non mi lusingar più speranza infida!

reprise:

> Non ti credo più, no!
> Colei che mi ferì
> d'amarmi si pentì;
> ad altro amante l'amore mio donò,
> e del mio fido cor fui l'omicida.
> Non mi lusingar più, speranza infida!

The duo *Non mi lusingar* (ex. XXIV) is a unique piece among the
ternary cantatas for reasons other than its text. If one were to judge the
form merely by its physical appearance in the source, the tendency would
be to see it as a ternary cantata whose first unit is constructed as an
envelope, thus: AbA' ://: c / A''bA' //. But the relationship between the
parts is not typical of the envelope design. The envelope setting (the
recapitulated first verse in the concluding passage of the first unit) is much
shorter than the introduction (the setting of the first verse)—seven measures compared to 20—and it is almost entirely recomposed (ex. XXIV,
mm. 38-44 and 1-20). Moreover, the introduction is an entity, itself the
length of the second unit (c). Although no double bar separates it from
the continuation of the first unit, it stands alone.

Following the initial statement of the second verse in the soprano
(mm. 20-22), the alto enters in imitation at the octave below and, while
the soprano continues until the seventh verse, reiterates the second verse
with an ostinato rhythmic motive almost up to the recapitulated opening

verse that concludes the first unit, thus holding the second through seventh verses together in a special way (see above, pp. 85-86).

The second unit alone, a little less than the length of the unit described above (mm. 21-44), cannot stand separated from the recapitulated first verse that follows it (mm. 65-77). Without it the second unit has neither an adequate length to balance against the preceding unit, nor an adequate conclusion. Its final phrase would be the transitional passage composed for the most part on the dominant pedal (measures 60-64), a passage that is more typical within a unit leading to the concluding segment than at the close of a unit. Significantly, the setting of the reprise verse following this transitional passage is neither a variant of the first setting (a fact which points to the exclusive, separate quality of the introduction, for it is heard but once), nor a quotation of the concluding passage of the first unit. The closure of the second unit begins with a new setting of the verse, and ends with a quotation of all but the first beats of the last phrase of the first unit. The relationship of the two ternary units by recurring cadences is not typical, less so the conclusion of both units with the same verse, but there are precedents for both: recurring cadences are also found in the ternary cantatas *Difenditi, o core* and *Soffrirei* and the quotation of the final verse of the first unit-refrain within the second unit is also a peculiar trait of the rondo *Hor guardate* (see above, p. 97).

The Ternary Design Within Larger Cantatas. Unlike the binary and rondo designs, the ternary design is seldom found forming a unit of an aria di più parti. In *Satiatevi, olà*, the one aria di più parti that does contain a unit composed like a ternary arietta, the compositional procedure is more characteristic of the envelope design than of the ternary. The text of this aria di più parti unit is like that of the ternary arietta *Disperate speranze*: the reprise is one verse, the second section is formed of five verses, the rhyme scheme is A bcbca A. The second section is distinguished from the first by a change of meter, a typical device of the ternary design; but unlike almost all ternary cantatas, the cadence preceding the second section is not to the tonic—the first section closes in the key of the dominant. The first section is recapitulated only in part; the arietta concludes with a new and extended setting of the opening verse that closes in the tonic—a trait of the envelope design, not of the ternary.

The Rounded Binary Form

There are 19 cantatas with a two-part design in which the close of the second part—both music and text—is identical to, or a variant of, the opening or the close of the first part.

At first glance the rounded binary cantatas may seem to belong to either the ternary or rondo groups. The recurrence of the reprise verse, the verse that usually both opens and closes the first unit and also concludes the second, suggests this relationship. But unlike the ternary and rondo reprise, that of the rounded binary design is not a separate, closed unit; it is incorporated into each of two larger units. With "A" representing the reprise verse and prime (') representing a variant and usually an extension of its first setting, the single rounded binary strophe is schematically: A b A' // c A' //. Among the four cantatas of one strophe[23] only the first unit of *Quante volte* lacks the envelope design—the first verse recurs only at the close of the second unit: A b // c A' //.

In this group of ariette corte there are two forms of strophic repetition. Five of the rounded binary cantatas have a strophic form in which both units are repeated with entirely new text—the kind of strophic repetition that is typical of the simple binary cantatas (see exx. IV and XI).[24] In the second kind of strophic design, the first unit is not repeated; additional text is given for the second unit only. The original reprise verse is retained, however, and concludes each new stanza: A b A' // c A' // c A' //.[25]

The near-total absence of strophic variation in the rounded binary cantatas is certainly not due to the absence of strophic texts (as it probably is in the ternary cantatas), for, as indicated above, 15 of the 19 cantatas have texts for the repetition of the second unit or of both units. Nor is the relative infrequency of arioso and recitative passages apparently the reason, for the one example of variation occurs in *Uscite di porto*, which is in 6/4. The cantata *Disperati*, whose first unit, an arioso, could undergo variation with the words of the second strophe, is instead left unvaried. A possible reason for the lack of variation is the literal recurrence of a substantial portion of the text, the chief feature of the rounded binary cantatas. Since Luigi tends to vary only those parts of a cantata whose text changes, he would normally leave the setting of a reprise unvaried. But in *Uscite di porto* he does the exceptional: in that portion of the second unit with new text, he varies the melodic line slightly, whereas in the concluding phrase with the reprise verse he makes substantial changes. It may be that the strophic variations in this cantata have survived because of this exceptional procedure. I am inclined to believe that in some of the cantatas of this group variations were improvised and not notated, or if notated, have not been preserved.

The strophic design of *Uscite di porto* (ex. VI), which is found in only one source, is misrepresented by the incorrect use of the designations "Prima" and "2a." The two segments of the first unit are labeled "Prima" and "2a"; the second unit is "3a" and the subsequent stanzas for the repetition of the second unit are "4a" and "5a." The mislabeling is probably due to the ritornello that sets off the introductory segment of the first unit. Since a ritornello rarely segments a unit but usually marks its close, the copyist surmised that a new unit began after the ritornello cadence. *Uscite di porto* is not a cantata of five parts but of four: the first and second unit and the two strophic repetitions of the latter.

In two other rounded binary cantatas having the same strophic design as *Uscite* the identical designations occur, but in different places. The second units of *Ohime, madre* and *M'uccidete* are marked "Pa" (prima), and the texts of the stanza for the strophic repetition of this unit are marked "2a" (seconda). This is misleading but logical—the first and second stanzas for the second unit are correctly identified as such. The designations are used as in the rondo cantatas for the second unit and its strophic repetition; the first unit, like the rondo first unit, is left unmarked.

Another use of "2a" occurs in the duo *Risolvetevi*, a rounded binary cantata of a single strophe (ex. XIII). Here the designation is used, as in the binary cantatas, for the second part of the two-part form.

A modification of the second strophic rounded binary design is found in *Mio core languisce*. The first unit is composed of an introductory verse and of the reprise verse. It is unique in the presentation of the reprise only after the introductory verse, and in the brevity of its text, a rhymed couplet. Although the second unit is formed of more verses than the first—six hexasyllables precede the reprise verse, in comparison to one— the two units receive settings that are nearly equal in length. The six hexasyllables preceding the quoted reprise conclusion are set tersely— they span 12 measures of 3/2. On the other hand, the single introductory verse of the first unit has a setting that extends to nearly ten measures of 3/2. With "x" representing the introductory passage, the form is x A// b A// b A// b A//.

Peculiar Traits. The distinctive trait of the rounded binary cantatas is the relationship of the two units by the quotation of a passage of the first unit at the conclusion of the second; in two of the 19 cantatas the quoted passage is the introductory segment, in the others it is the concluding segment. In 13 of the 17 cantatas where the quoted passage is the conclusion of the first unit, the quotation is exact or almost exact.[26] There are only two instances where a slight change occurs in the opening measure of the reprise. The change in *Ohime* is due to the different tonal goal preceding the reprise; in *Mio cor* it results from musical enjambement with the preceding phrase. In *Mio core*, too, some melodic variation occurs in the closing phrase of the second and third strophes. One of the MS sources of *Difenditi, amore* slightly extends the quotation, which uniquely includes both the close of the first unit and its beginning, making it more climactic by the interpolation of several beats.[27] The four other cantatas that end with a reference to the close of the first unit alter the passage substantially in the process.[28] This procedure of altering quoted material is an earmark of Luigi's style. The changes are of different kinds, as a discussion of the four cantatas will illustrate.

In *Uscite di porto* (ex. VI) the reprise conclusion and its strophic repetitions are related to the concluding segment of the first unit as its strophic variations. While retaining the bass, Luigi composes a completely new melody (see first ending). But this concluding passage is not quoted exactly at the close of the subsequent strophes. The first strophic repetition retains the beginning of the new melody and quotes the last part of the original setting. One new measure joins the two segments (see second ending). The concluding passage of the third strophe is the shortest. It begins with the concluding segment of the first strophe, but curtails it and closes abruptly with the "Speranza" cadence (third ending). It is typical that the ritornello concluding the other sections is omitted at the close of the last.

Another procedure is used in *Sei pur dolce*, the second of four cantatas whose final passage is related to the close of the first without exact quotation. In *Sei pur dolce* reference to the introductory and concluding passages of the first unit, which are essentially the same (ex. 5a and b), is made in several ways: the final passage recalls the head of its models, with a new harmonic realization; quotes rhythmic motives; closes with a variant of the cadence to G minor; and is the same length (compare exx. 5 and 101). The five measures of this final setting of the reprise verse, however, are articulated quite differently. In the original setting the first gesture, to B-flat, is terse, and the longer cadential movement, realized sequentially and melismatically, is to G minor. In the concluding setting the first is the broader of the two cadential segments—the cadence to B-flat comes a whole measure later than in the original setting. But despite its brevity, the final cadence has a strong conclusive quality emphasized by the presence of the chord of the lowered second degree, its only appearance in the cantata. Whereas the melodic line of the introductory-closing passage of the first unit is composed of three successive peaks—F, D and C, each reached by a stepwise ascent of the third, and a final contour that descends from the dominant to the tonic—the new melodic line stresses the continuous descent from the first peak, F, at its opening, to the tonic G, a seventh below. It does this in gradual stages, through a series of descending thirds. One hears clearly E-flat-C, then D-B-flat, then finally B-flat-G. The two melodic contours, though employing the same tones and similar rhythmic motives and descending from F to G, are finely differentiated.

The third of the four cantatas, whose final passage quotes only in part from the concluding segment of the first unit, poses a problem. *Armatevi di sdegno* is found in only one source and there the entire second unit is without text. Despite this fact, however, it is possible to identify the design as a rounded binary. The first unit is formed the usual way with a variant setting of the first verse at the close (see ex. 17a and b, p. 143). The textless second unit concludes with a period that begins with three measures quoted from the final segment of the first unit, followed by five measures of new music related rhythmically to the two previous settings of the reprise verse. The verse fits the music perfectly; that its recurrence was intended is extremely likely (ex. 102).

The derivation of the final passage of *Non mi fate* (ex. XI) illustrates still another procedure. The exact quotation that concludes the second unit is prefaced by the transposition of the cantata's initial theme in the key of the relative major, thereby making the final period one of three segments formed in the typical Rossian manner. This closure actually quotes the introductory passage of the cantata, but since the introductory passage transposed to the key of the minor dominant also concludes the first unit, the final quoted and extended reprise setting is related to both the opening and close of the first unit.

Quante volte and *Rendetevi*, whose first units of text do not conclude with the opening verse, are the two exceptions (noted earlier) in which the reprise ending refers to the opening of the first unit instead of to its close. In both cantatas an additional phrase extends the quoted passage. In *Quante volte* the entire opening passage with its Phrygian cadence is followed by a concluding phrase half its length. In *Rendetevi* the additional passage—nearly the length of the quoted one—precedes the contracted and varied introductory period. The changes are a result of reworking the first segment with an elision of the third and fourth measures. The bass is newly-composed throughout the quoted phrase.

Since the earmark of the rounded form is the identity or near-identity of the closing segments of the two units, one may question the inclusion of *Rendetevi* and *Quante volte* in this group. In both cases it can be shown that musical correspondences have been introduced even though the usual textual recurrences are absent.

In *Rendetevi*, despite differences in rhythm and bass line, the final phrases of both units refer to the introductory passage. A recurring cadence relates the three segments (ex. 103). It is noteworthy that the final cadence (ex. 103c) quotes the melody of the first cadence (ex. 103a), and the bass of the second (with rhythmic adjustments, ex. 103b). The second bass is a typical prolongation bass and thus a more fitting close.

Despite their more substantial melodic differences, the final cadences of the two units of *Quante volte* (ex. 104) are as much related as those of *Rendetevi*. The melodic line of one cadence fits the bass of the other; moreover, if both melodies are combined (ex. 104c), it can be seen that they are merely the separate parts of a single cadential suspension figure.

Apart from a tendency towards metrical similarity, the correspondences between the two units of the rounded binary design do not normally extend beyond the concluding segment of the cantata and some portion of the first unit. A more extensive relationship between the two parts is evident only in *Uscite di porto* (ex. VI): both units begin with an introductory gesture that establishes the tonality B-flat. The phrases are similarly composed of two balancing segments; the second phrase of the second unit is the same as the phrase following the introductory segment of the first unit ("fortuna agl'audaci e scorta fedele" and "indarno co' pianti cercate"). Moreover, the fourth phrase, which leads to the conclusion of the second unit—a phrase cadencing in C minor—recalls the phrase heard in the corresponding place of the first unit—in G minor. The technique is one that Luigi uses in some arie di più parti to relate the different successive units, but it is not prevalent in the short closed cantatas.

Problems in Determining Whether the Design is Rondo or Rounded Binary. *Respira, core* (ex. V), included among the rounded binary cantatas, appears to be a rondo because the rubric "da capo" with a musical incipit recalling the opening of the first unit occurs at the end of the second unit. Performed as the rubric requires, with a refrain of 36 measures of 3/4 (compared to a second unit of 20 measures), the cantata would have an unbalanced, atypical rondo design—the refrain is disproportionately longer than the second unit.

A conceivable solution to the problem is the recapitulation of the concluding segment of the first unit, which is a setting of the first verse. This, as we have seen, is the typical way of forming the conclusion of the rounded binary design. In fact, there are several clues that suggest that this is possibly a correct solution. The last phrase of the second unit (mm. 54-57), as it stands without reprise, is transitional in character. It follows a melismatic cadential passage to the minor dominant that seems to be an important structural goal—a phrase on the dominant pedal preceding it emphasizes its significance. The melody of the transitional passage is also contained within the opening phrase of the concluding passage of the first unit, where it also succeeds a cadence to the minor dominant (mm. 24-26). The parallelism may be significant: in each case a strong B minor cadence proceeds through G major back to the tonic E minor, and the concluding segments in both utilize the same melody. Thus the transitional phrase leading to the reprise at the end of the second unit would, if we accept this solution, be followed by a brief echo effect corresponding to the rhyme of the verses "prendi vigore, respira, core!" With the second unit concluded in this manner, the result is a rounded binary design whose two units are well balanced: 36 and 33 measures.

Another solution, one which is perhaps more musical, would be the omission of the first three measures that duplicate the closing melody of the transitional passage. Measure 57 of the second unit leads smoothly to measure 27, the fourth measure of the concluding segment of the first unit. The result is excellent: the final passage is of two parts, the first leading to a semi-cadence, the second leading to the tonic with a melismatic prolongation cadence—a fitting conclusion. Though musically feasible, neither this nor the previous hypothesis is supported by any evidence from the sources. Hence we cannot dismiss the possibility that the cantata is a rondo after all.

In the copy of the cantata appended (ex. V), the various possibilities of its performance are indicated: (1) the ending in the sources recalling the whole of the first unit; (2) the first possibility suggested in its realization as a rounded binary cantata—the recapitulation of the concluding segment of the first unit; and (3) the second possibility—the recapitulation of all but the first three measures of the concluding segment of the first unit.

A case similar to *Respira* is the cantata *Su, su, mio core*. The rubric "da capo" at the close of the second unit most probably signifies the recapitulation not of the whole first unit, but of its concluding segment only. The second unit as it is—a passage of seven-and-one-half measures of 6/8—does not balance the much longer first unit of 21 measures of the same meter. No sequences, melismas, or repetitions give the second unit length; but this austerity is common in the first segment of a concluding binary unit. What is required is a concluding segment after the cadence to the supertonic D minor. Significantly, the same cadence is heard in the first unit preceding its conclusion; the parallelism suggests that both units conclude with the same passage. It seems to me that the form A b A' // c A' // is intended.

In three of the sources and in Riemann's published copy, the second unit of *Difenditi, amore*, like that of *Su, su* and *Respira*, is followed by a rubric that recalls the entire opening unit. Riemann, in fact, gives *Difenditi* as an example of a "da Capo-Aria." But the opening unit is more than twice the length of the three phrases that lead to the minor mediant cadence. The proportions are not at all typical of the rondo or ternary designs. Here too it seems that the rubric indicates the da capo of only a segment of the first part. Because of the unusual length of the introductory passage (the first setting of the recurring verse) and its self-contained character—it begins with a concitato passage and closes with double cadences to the tonic—it, rather than the shorter concluding segment, fits the second unit as its conclusion. The concluding segment of the first unit is too short to give the second unit its needed length. With such evidence in the music, I determined the form to be A b A' // c A // c A // c A //. Fortunately, proof of the correctness of this decision is found in a fourth source, the MS *I* Rvat, Barb, 4175. Here the strophe concludes with the reprise of the opening setting of the first verse (ex. III).

At first glance, *Non mi fate mentire* (ex. XI) seems a miniature rondo. Its poetic design A bba A cca A might be considered a variant of the usual rondo design—the refrain, one verse instead of four, the second and third units, three verses of unequal length, and asymmetric. But the rondo appearance is superficial. Unlike any rondo, the whole piece is repeated strophically with an entirely new text.[29] Also, in the anonymous solo version, a double bar follows the second statement of the reprise verse, dividing the cantata into two parts: the first, a stanza of five verses with the typical design of the rounded binary first unit: AbbaA, and the second, a concluding quatrain with the recurrence of the reprise verse: ccaA.

Musically the binary design is clearly delineated. Except for the dominant goal of the first unit—it is the rare binary cantata that terminates elsewhere than the tonic—the tonal scheme is typical. The tonic is established in the opening phrase, the penultimate goal of both units is the dominant, and that of the final phrase is the tonic. The proportions are normal as well. And typically, the three settings of the recurring verse are related.[30]

An anonymous version of the same text for two sopranos seems to be related to Luigi's setting. The closing segment of the first unit begins as a quotation of the introductory passage at the fourth below, just as in Luigi's cantata, but the quotation is broken in the ninth measure and the phrase terminates with a new cadential segment. The reprise at the close of the second unit relates explicitly to the close of Luigi's cantata, for it quotes its opening phrase (ex. XI, following Luigi's piece). The quoted segment is extended and then followed by the last three measures of the first unit, thus relating the two units in the usual way. In this cantata, too, the final passage is preceded by a Phrygian cadence to the dominant.

The Rounded Binary Design Within the Arie di Più Parti. Among the arie di più parti, I know of only two that contain a unit composed as a rounded binary arietta. *Torna indietro* begins with the form and *Noi siam* closes with it. The two ariettas are quite different in mood and in the structure of their parts. The one in *Noi siam* is simpler and more homogeneous in style. It is meant to be a song. Seeing the shadows of the night darkening the sky, the girls cease chatting about their boyfriends and decide, "Torniamo all'albergo, torniam si, ma cantando!" They return home singing a song about the trouble they have for sale, about the heartaches they are ready to give. Their song is a rounded binary arietta.

The text of the first section has the common design: AbbaA; the second section has two symmetric stanzas (the text is the second type of strophic form) with the common rhyme scheme: cddceffaA. That the verses are all octosyllables may account for the fact that the meter remains 6/4 from begining to end. The first part is regularly composed—the concluding passage is in part quoted from the first setting, in part newly composed, and each of the two settings of the reprise verse is longer than the inner segment. A new feature is the double strophe design of the second unit and its two stanzas. The second stanza is not set strophically to the music of the first, but it is in part variation, in part newly composed. The second setting is related closely to the first structurally. Both begin with an ostinato segment whose motive is borrowed from the reprise. The ostinato in both is broken with a cadence to the mediant, D minor; and both precede the concluding passage they share with a cadence to G minor, the tonal goal that also precedes the conclusion of the first unit. The reprise—the conclusion of each of the three parts—terminates with double cadences to the tonic B-flat and a ritornello that repeats the bass of the preceding cadence.

The recurring opening verse of *Torna indietro* (ex. XXII) introduces a recitative-arioso that forms the main part of the first unit; this inner segment is much more substantial than that in *Noi siam*. The closing segment of this first part is composed in the usual manner: the opening hendecasyllable is recapitulated and its setting quotes from the introductory passage, extends it and closes with a ritornello. The second part of the arietta is made of several segments. It begins with a recitative that leads to a short aria in duple meter. This, in turn, is followed by a passage in triple meter set to hexasyllables. The arietta concludes with the recapitulation of the closing segment of the first unit.

Summary. Although the texts of the rounded binary cantatas are similar to those of the ternary and rondo groups—the one exception being the recurrence of the opening (and, usually, last) verse of the first unit at the close of the second—the musical designs do not correspond. Despite major differences between them, the rounded binary form is more nearly like the simple binary.

The first unit essentially resembles the first units of the other three groups: it begins with an introductory passage announcing the primary tonality; it is usually unsegmented by metric, stylistic or tempo changes; its range of modulation is generally smaller than that of the second unit; it is approximately the same length as the second unit (more usually somewhat shorter than somewhat longer); and it concludes with a strong cadential passage reaffirming the tonic, occasionally reinforced by a ritornello. But an identifying trait, observable in only a minority of the ternary and rondo first units and in very few simple binary first units, is the envelope design with which 16 of the 19 rounded binary cantatas begin. The closing passage of the first unit refers back to the introduction, quoting it either entirely or partially with changes that make the passage a more fitting conclusion.

The second unit, like that of the simple binary, also concludes with a strong cadential gesture in the tonic key, and the setting of the final verse and its repetitions is, in the majority of the cantatas, equal to or greater in length than the preceding segment of the unit. But neither the binary nor the ternary and rondo second units shares the qualifying characteristic of the rounded binary second unit. The final passage either quotes the concluding passage of the first unit or it is the same as the opening passage. A clearcut cadence immediately precedes this concluding segment, as in the simple binary cantatas. However, one of the distinguishing traits of the simple binary design, the recitative passage that leads to the concluding aria segment, is absent in all but one rounded binary arietta. Segmentation of the second unit by metric contrast, a characteristic of many of the simple binary pieces, is rare in the rounded binary second units. Perhaps significantly, this group of cantatas also shows a tendency towards metrical similarity between the two units, thus further distinguishing it from the other cantata types. In all other respects, however, the units of the rounded binary design are as clearly differentiated as those of the other groups.

Finally, there are two types of strophic form in this group of cantatas. The majority of the cantatas are strophically extended in a way that is peculiar to this group alone: the first unit is performed once, while the second unit is repeated successively with new text (except for the concluding verse, which is the original reprise verse). The strophic repetition of the entire cantata with new text—the typical strophic form of the simple binary and ternary cantatas—is found in only a few rounded binary pieces.

Notes

Notes for Introduction

1. Further information is given in my article "Luigi Rossi," *The New Grove Dictionary of Music and Musicians*, 1980, vol. XVI, pp. 217-221.

2. During the seventeenth century the fluid designations "aria," "arietta," "cantata," "canzone," "canzonetta," "madrigale," and "recitativo," while rarely appearing in the manuscripts, are found in titles of printed collections. Some of these designations refer to style, not to specific forms; thus I do not distinguish between them, but include all under the general category "cantata." By "cantata" then I mean the broad category of vocal chamber music for one or more voices and continuo comprising a variety of stylistic and formal species. A survey of the use of the term is found in Gloria Rose, "The Cantatas of Carissimi" (unpublished Ph.D. dissertation, Yale University, 1959), pp. 22-25.

3. See Appendix: Musical Sources, Manuscripts in Volume 2 .

4. Luigi Rossi was often called simply by his Christian name, as was the custom for musicians, virtuosi, artists, and poets who had endeared themselves to their contemporaries. The attribution "Luigi" is found in many of the manuscripts, and reference to "Luigi" is made in letters of Della Valle, Charles de Saint-Evremond, Pierre Bourdelot, Atto Melani, Elpidio Benedetti, in the correspondance between Thomas Gobert and Constantin Huyghens, and in the encomiastic sonnet by Charles D'Assoucy. See Alberto Ghislanzoni, *Luigi Rossi* (Milan: Fratelli Bocca, 1954), pp. 55, 173, 150, 180, 191, 127, 123 and 127, and 199 respectively.

5. Alberto Ghislanzoni, *Luigi Rossi*, pp. 40-56.

6. Manfred Bukofzer, *Music in the Baroque Era* (New York: Norton, 1947), p. 120. The example Bukofzer quotes is not Luigi's; it is taken from *Del silentio il giogo* (Thematic Index 2, no. 318), which cannot be attributed to Luigi either on bibliographical or stylistic grounds. Parts of this same cantata are quoted and the cantata discussed as a model of Luigi's compositions in this genre in Claude Palisca's *Baroque Music* (Englewood: Prentice-Hall, 1968), pp. 106-108.

7. Since this study was completed, five of the cantatas included in this number have proven to be Marco Marazzoli's, and one, possibly Pasqualini's. They are marked in the tables of cantatas. Also, the 294 cantatas do not include *Ho voto di non amare, Chi consiglia un dubbio* and *Non ti doler, mio core*. These cantatas attributed to Luigi Rossi were found after my study was completed. They are included in Thematic In-

dex 1 and in the first table. The statistics throughout my text do not exclude the six spurious cantatas, nor do they include the three newly found ones.

8. The cantatas are listed both in a continuous alphabetical table, pp. 185-191, and in separate tables according to the formal groups named above, pp. 192-198. One cantata, *Adagio, speranza*, is not included in any of the six groups; this strophic arietta of a single unsegmented unit is listed only in the continuous alphabetical table.

9. The lost cantata *Sola fra i suoi* is included among the seventeen. (Regarding this cantata, see Thematic Index 2, no. 384.) Not counted is the version of *Sparsa il crine* found in I Rvat, Chigi Q VIII 99 (see Thematic Index 1, no. 185).

10. Margaret Murata, "Further Remarks on Pasqualini," *Analecta Musicologica*, XIX (1976), pp. 135-136, and Gloria Rose, "The Cantatas of Carissimi," use the term "composite" for an aria di più parti.

11. Concerning *S'era alquanto*, see pp. 131-32, n. 17.

12. Giovanni Lotti, *Poesie Latine e Toscane* (Roma: Gio.Giacomo Komarek bohemo, 1688); for example, I, p. 103 and II, p. 37.

13. *Pria ch'al sdegno, Perche speranze, Quando mi chiede, Sospiri miei, Spiega un volo, Sovra un lido* and *Atra notte*.

14. Ghislanzoni, *Luigi Rossi*, p. 53: ". . .si chi i limiti tra un tipo e l'altro non sempre riescono precisabili e spesso riesce arduo incasellare le singole produzioni rossiane in uno dei tre tipi strutturali (Cantata-Aria, Cantata con Refrain e Cantata a Rondo) riconosciuti dalla musicologia più recente (ad es. da M. Bukofzer in *Music in the Baroque Era*, New York, 1947)."

15. I.e., binary, rondo, and rounded binary cantatas. Among the ternary cantatas there is no example of strophic variation.

16. It cannot be proven, for example, that Carissimi invented the double strophe form since Luigi's cantatas *Attra notte* and *Sovra un lido* are perhaps earlier examples than "Se il mio core" from *Scrivete, occhi dolenti*, one of Carissimi's arie di più parti. Another example that may have been composed before *Scrivete* is Carlo Caproli's *Hor ch'il ciel di stelle adorno*.

17. Ghislanzoni, *Luigi Rossi*, pp. 32, 56, 123, 158.

18. *Ibid.*, pp. 54 (Bonini), 55 (Della Valle), 59 and 60 (Doni), 91 (Atto Melani), 123 (Huyghens), 173 (Saint-Evremond), 176 (Perti and Berardi), 180 (Brossard), 192 (Cardinal d'Este), 199 (Charles D'Assoucy) and 200 (Margherita Costa). Gloria Rose, "The Cantatas of Carissimi," pp. 14 (Bonini, not the passage Ghislanzoni quotes), 16 (Perti, the passage from which Ghislanzoni quotes is here given in full), 17 (Christoph Bernhard), 18, 19 (Abbé Francois Raguenet). Romand Rolland, *Musiciens d'Autrefois* (Paris: Librarie Hachette, 1908), p. 70 (Brossard, le Cerf de la Vieville de Fresneuse and Benigne de Bacilly). The composers Antonio Cesti and Anton Francesco Tenaglia also paid tribute to the master, the former in his cantata *Aspettate*—see David Burrows,

The Italian Cantata I, Antonio Cesti (Wellesley College, 1964) p. ix; and the latter in *Che volete chi'io canti*.

Notes for Chapter 1

1. In the cantatas *Che dici*, *Che vuoi*, *Chi di voi*, *Chi mi credeva*, *Chi non sa*, *Ch'io speri* and many others.

2. The comparison occurs in *Farfalletta* and *Al bel lume*.

3. *Olà, pensieri*, *Chi trovasse*, *Se non corre*, *Sospiri, su, su*.

4. The verse "Non amar tanto, no!" occurs in both *Quante volte* and *Se nell'arsura* as refrain. In the latter, a binary piece, it comes at the close of the first section of each strophe, an unusual place for a refrain. It proleptically announces the final verse and refrain, a rewording of the admonition in the positive form "Ama poco, ama poco!"

5. *The Poetical Works of William Drummond of Hawthornden*, ed. L. E. Kastner. (Manchester: University Press, 1913), I, 17.

6. "Spirti" here means "spiriti vitali"—life-giving incorporeal substances.

7. The text continues, "se al canto un duro coro non si può frangere." In the anonymous cantata *Che volete ch'io canti* (US CHH, Music Vault M2. 1 M1, ff. 45-50) whose text continues, "mi sento infreddato; il suono è scordato," the singer is critical of the fashionable modes of singing.

8. Burrows, *The Italian Cantata*, vol. I, pp. 70-93. David Burrows translates Sebastiano Baldini's text, p. xv. In a similar cantata, *L'Astratto*, by Barbara Strozzi, the singer-lover's text also treats of the diverse modes of addressing the beloved in song, and of the power of music. See Ellen Rosand, "Barbara Strozzi," *JAMS*, 1978, p. 271.

9. A musician-lover is the protagonist of the arietta *E che cantar poss'io* (Thematic Index 1, no. 66).

10. The quality and mood of the original text is entirely betrayed in the translation published in *Gems of Antiquity*, ed. Otto Neitzel (Cincinatti: The John Church Co., 1909).

11. The unusual quality of this text may be due to its operatic origin. Luigi's text is taken from Marco da Gagliano's opera *Flora*.

12. The closing strophic arietta "Su, sperate, o mie pupille" of *Ombre fuggite*.

13. Ghislanzoni, *Luigi Rossi*, pp. 32, 69, 121.

14. It seems relevant to note that none of Luigi's cantatas involves either of the two popular heroines, Dido and Ariadne.

15. This is true of most of Luigi's contemporaries. Ellen Rosand relates of Barbara Strozzi's cantatas that they are "confined primarily to the expression of a single affect: the

suffering . . . caused by unrequited love." Rosand, "Barbara Strozzi," *JAMS* (1978), p. 262.

16. A strophe of admonition is not an infrequent conclusion to an aria di più parti. Similar to the strophe quoted, the conclusion of the anonymous aria di più parti *Era la notte e con horror profondo* begins "Apprendete, o voi mortali, quanti mali il mondo da!" (*I* Nc, 33.4.17, II, ff. 63-73v).

17. One finds it even in the cantatas whose protagonist is the desperate lover; in *Sassi, ch'or qui tra le ruine* (Thematic Index 2, no. 374), a text attributed to Marino, the last line of the fourth quatrain is almost that of *Piangea l'aurora*: "Ch'ogni cosa qua giú passa e non dura." Also "Cadente belta" is the subject of the anonymous ostinato arietta *Amanti, fuggite* (*F* Pbn, Vm7 4, ff. 42-44). Other cantatas whose texts treat of the fleetingness of beauty, youth and time are cited by David Burrows, "The Cantatas of Antonio Cesti" (unpublished Ph.D. dissertation, Brandeis University, 1961), p. 24.

18. "Caduco manto" Tasso calls the body in his poem *Quasi celeste Diva*. The adjective "caduco" seems to occur more than any other in descriptions of this kind; for example, in *Nel dì* the penitent confesses: "Di caduca bellezza un guardo, un riso furono il mio diletto."

19. Firenze, Galleria Pitti. Print by Innocenti, no. 572.

20. Probably the fame and beauty of the music suggested the idea of giving the text a religious slant so that it might be sung in a convent.

21. The influence of Battista Guarini's *Il Pastor Fido* (published 1589) on the form as well as the diction and content of Seicento poetry is evident in the use of the signatory expression "Ma che pro?". In cantata and opera texts it is used in the same way as in the literary model: at the close of an impassioned soliloquy where the words mark a change in the thought of the protagonist. See Margaret Murata, "The Recitative Soliloquy," *JAMS* XXXII (1979), p. 48.

22. We find towards the end of Monteverdi's *Lamento di Arianna*: "Cosí va, chi troppo ama e troppo crede!"; the final verse of Luigi's *Tra romite*: "Così va chi si fida!"; the refrain of *Così va*: "Così va, dice il mio core, in amore chi più serve manco fa!"; and the closing couplet of *Pensoso, afflitto*: "In amor così va: Beltà ch'affanna/ più che adorarsi vede è più tiranna." The exclamation is repeated often in the "aria allegro" towards the end of the long anonymous cantata *Partita Filli abbandonando Ergasto* (Nc, 33.4.14, II, pp. 193-228).

23. Examples besides those cited occur in *Mezza tra viva*, Olimpia's lament (see Thematic Index 2, no. 350), *Che ti resta* (see Thematic Index 2, no. 310), Luigi's *E che cantar* and *Hor che avvolte* (the exclamation here is "Ma che mi giova?") and in the anonymous cantata *Spuntava il dí*; see above, page 19.

24. *I* Bc, Q47, ff. 8v-94v.

25. One finds in Marino for example: "Ecco il monte, ecco il sasso, ecco lo speco," *Opere* (Napoli, 1961), p. 507; and "Il valor, lo splendor, la fede, il zelo," *La Lira, Rime* (Venetia, 1629), vol. III.

26. See also *Ahi, quante volte* and *Con amor* quoted above, pp. 10 and 14.

27. The texts of *Sognai, Quando spiega, Chiuda quest'occhi, All'ombra, Atra notte, S'era alquanto* and *Horche in notturna pace*.

28. The texts of *Se non corre, Già nel oblio, Mentre sorge, Ne notte ne dì, Ombre fuggite, All'hor* and *Horche notte guerriera*.

29. The quotations that are unidentified are those that coincide or begin with the first verse of the cantata.

30. Maurice Valency, *In Praise of Love* (New York: Macmillan, 1958), pp. 25-26.

31. Ibid, p. 6.

Notes for Chapter 2

1. Nine of the rondos have three musical units—*Augellin, Mi, contento, Non la volete, Non sarà, Occhi ardenti, Sospiri, su, su, Speranze, che dite, Speranze, sentite, Sulla veglia*.

2. See listing on note 1 above.

3. Thirty-five of the 121 binary cantatas.

4. Thirty-nine cantatas.

5. The quatrain forms one or both units in 86 binary cantatas; in 47, the first unit; in 14, the second; in 25, both.

6. Each letter represents a verse; the recurrence of a letter signifies rhyme relationship between the verses represented by the same letter; upper case means recapitulation of the verse.

7. *Mai finirò*, one of the seven binary cantatas that begin with an envelope design, has the text of a rounded binary cantata—its opening verse, recapitulated at the close of the first unit, also recurs at the close of the second. The musical setting, however, is not a rounded binary design because the setting of the recapitulated verse at the end of the cantata is in no way related to either of its settings in the first unit; thus the qualifying feature of the rounded form is missing. The musical design is simple binary.

8. Forty-two of the strophic binary cantatas.

9. This type of verse recurrence is exceptionally found in four strophic rondo cantatas (*Fate quel, Libertà, Ne notte,* and *Speranze, che dite*). Here too the last verse (or couplet) of the second unit returns unchanged at the close of the subsequent stanzas; thus these cantatas have two refrains—the rondo refrain proper and the refrain concluding the various stanzas of the second unit: A bC A bC A bC//.

10. The portions bracketed are those not included in the respective versions.

11. Seventy-five texts are of mixed verses, 125 are entirely of unmixed pari or impari and 15 are almost entirely of pari.

12. Of the 94 texts that comprise these three groups, 50 are entirely or almost entirely of pari verses and 12 are entirely of impari; the rest, 32, are of mixed verses. Of the 121 binary texts, 16 are entirely or almost entirely of pari verses and 62 are entirely of impari; the rest, 43, are of mixed verses.

13. Only three of the cantatas of three musical units (see p. 119, note 1), *Non la volete*, *Augellin* and *Sospiri, su, su*, have symmetrically formed texts, texts that could have been set as strophic rondos.

14. The rondo begins with the opening quatrain as refrain; but following each of the subsequent units, this refrain is curtailed to a single couplet. See above, p. 101, for further discussion of this cantata.

15. The cantatas whose two units are not separated by any notational mark are the binary *Amor così*, *Amor s'io*, *Armatevi d'orgoglio*, *A tanti*, *De la vita*, *Dissi un giorno*, *Io ero*, *Precorrea*, *Quando spiega*, *Questo piccol*, *Ragion*, *Se nell'arsura*, *Tenti*; the rounded binary *Non mi fate mentire* and the rondos *Occhi ardenti* and *Adorate* (in one source without division marks, in the others with the usual double bars).

16. In a few rounded binary cantatas the closing segment of the second unit is not written out but a rubric directs the performer to quote from the first unit. The rubric in some cases does not specify the closing segment of the first unit, but seems to mean a return to its beginning and a recapitulation of it entirely. This problem is treated in chapter 3, pp. 110-12.

17. *Amor giura*, *Che cosa mi dice*, *Chi non ha*, *Così va*, *E chi non*.

18. A case in point is the version of *Si, v'ingannate* in the MS *I* G1, A.5.Cass. The strophic repetition of the second unit of the rondo is written out immediately following its first statement with no hint of the refrain recurring between them. The refrain returns only after the second strophe. The form definitely seems to be A b b A. But in all the other sources of the cantata the return of the refrain after the first strophe is very clearly indicated; in fact, in *GB* Och, 949 it is written out.

19. Burrows, *The Italian Cantata* vol. I, p. 88, measures 263-265. Ghislanzoni, *Luigi Rossi*, p. 92, points out the derivation of Estreviglio from the Spanish "estribillo," the refrain of Spanish songs then in vogue, but he is mistaken in considering the term a familiar name for Marc'Antonio Pasqualini (see Introduction, Volume 2, note 37).

20. Barring is erratic in almost all the manuscripts—6/4, 3/4 and 6/8 measures intermingle as do 6/2, 3/2 and 3/1, 3/2 and 6/4, 6/8 and 3/8.

21. Only 19 cantatas are composed entirely in 6/8. Regarding the relationship of this meter to hexasyllable and exhortative texts, see above, p. 53.

22. Cantatas or portions of cantatas in duple meter are generally in 4/4; measures of 2/4 are rare.

23. In some of the 30 texts of mixed verses composed without metric change there is no significant contrast of poetic meter between the two units; the different verse lengths intermingle without suggesting metric contrast.

24. This is not a convention in the other three formal types, but occurs in them exceptionally, and is generally text-motivated. In the rondo *Libertà*, for example, the second unit concludes with verses that recur as a refrain in the stanzas for its strophic repetition, as in some of the strophic binary cantatas. In the ternary *Non c'è che dire*, the second unit is a miniature binary arietta with all the traits of the binary design, text and music; and in the rondos *Che dici* and *Ne notte* the second units conclude, like those of binary pieces, with a hendecasyllable.

25. See above, p. 61.

26. These changes to duple meter are infrequent: the first happens at the close of the second units of *Che dici*, *Cor dolente* and the rondo of the aria di più parti *Da perfida*; the second, at the end of the refrain of *Nessun* and twice in the rondo of the aria di più parti *Se mi volete*. Related to these changes is the unique one at the close of the first unit of *E d'amore*. The unbarred measures of the ritornello contrast in harmonic rhythm, accent placement and tempo with the concluding phrases preceding it. Here, however, the change from the retarded movement in long notes of the last phrases to the measured movement in halves and quarters of the ritornello seems to be a change from triple to duple that indicates a quickening of the tempo rather than a retardation.

27. In these three groups more than half of the cantatas where metric change occurs are settings of mixed verses (25 of 40), whereas in the binary group the ratio is less than a third (24 of 66).

28. Seventeen of the 47 rondo and ternary texts of unmixed verses are composed with metric change. In these cantatas there is usually only one metric contrast, that differentiating the two units.

29. Omitting the 16 that are entirely in duple meter, all but ten of the binary cantatas conclude in triple meter—95.

30. Examples of such metric changes determined by the text are in the cantatas *Amanti*, *ardire*, *Amor con dolce*, *Che cosa*, *Che dici*, *Fan battaglia*, *Horche di marte*, *Non mi fate*, *O biondi*, *Occhi ardenti*, *Quand'io credo*, *Querelatevi*, *Si v'ingannate* and *Tu sarai*.

31. The pairing of 6/8 with hexasyllables is found in *Amor, e perche*, *Begl'occhi, pietà*, *Che cosa*, *Che dici, mio core*, *Ch'io speri*, *Deh, soffri*, *Difendi, mio core*, *Difenditi, amore*, *Due labbra*, *Fanciulla son io*, *Guardatevi, olà*, *La bella più bella*, *Mi contento cosi*, *Mio core, impara*, *Mai no'l'dirò*, *Nessun sene vanti*, *O biondi*, *Sparite dal core*, *Speranze, che dite*, *Su, su, su, mio core*, *Tu giuri*.

32. Examples of this correlation can be seen in *Il contento*, *Pietà, spietati* (ex. XXI), *Su, su, begl'occhi* and *Un cor che*. Although common in the music of Luigi and his contemporaries—much more so than in the music of the following generation—the relationship is obviously not a consistent one. For example, the first unit of *Un cor*, a

setting of octosyllables, is in 6/8, whereas *A te*, entirely in duple meter and in aria style, contains no octosyllable, but consists wholly of impari verses.

33. *A me stesso*, *Chi non sa*, *Cosi va*, *E chi non*, *Fate quel*, *Hor guardate*, and *O cieli*.

34. Triple meter, or compound meter, the key of B-flat and hexasyllables are conjoined in the cantatas *A la rota*, *Amanti, sentite*, *Bella bocca*, *Che non puote*, *Chi puo*, *Corilla*, *Difenditi, amore*, *Due labbra*, *Fanciulla*, *Ho voto*, *Libertà*, *Noi siam*, *Non più gioie*, *Sempre dunque*, *Se non corre*, *Sopra conca*, *Vienmi*, *Vorrei*.

35. The binary *Dissi un giorno* and the rounded binary *Non mi fate*.

36. The binary *Il cor mi dice*, *Io che sin*, *Partii* and *Tu giuri*, the ternary *Mortale che pensi*, and the rondo cantatas *A chi lasso*, *Chi trovasse*, *Come penare*, *E chi non* and *Che dici*. The refrain, closing with a Phrygian cadence, regularly concludes all but the last of these cantatas. The final cadence of the refrain of the rondo of the aria di più parti *V'è, v'è* is also Phrygian.

37. *Mortale, che pensi*, *A chi, lasso* and *Che dici*. The same relationship is apparent at the close of the refrain of *V'è, v'è*.

38. The one exception is the binary arietta *Come tosto*, one of the shortest, and probably one of the earliest, of Luigi's cantatas, that uniquely begins in one tonality and ends in another—the first unit begins and ends in F major; the second moves to D minor.

39. The tonal area is usually most restricted in the shortest cantatas. *Io che sin*, for example, moves no further than the dominant key. In *Il cor mi dice*, *Luci belle* and *Partii* the tonal range includes only two keys other than the tonic: the relative major and minor subdominant in the first, the supertonic and subdominant in the second and the relative major and its dominant in the third. *Come tosto*, however, despite its brevity touches upon three tonalities beyond the primary one: the relative major, minor subdominant and dominant.

40. Cadences to the subdominant are less frequent than those to the dominant and relative major or the relative minor, but there are some extraordinary movements to the subdominant, especially in the closing segments of the binary cantatas. At the close of *Gelosia*, for example, the return to the tonic, C minor, from E-flat is made through a modulation to the subdominant, which is also realized with a subdominant pivot. The minor dominant of E-flat, B-flat minor, becomes subdominant in F minor.

41. If the second unit does not begin with a modulation, the tendency is for the first phrase to lead to the dominant chord with a Phrygian cadence.

42. See *Disperati* (ex. IV, m. 53), *Lungi da me* (ex. XX, m. 44), *Quanto è credulo* (ex. XXVI, m. 12), *Respira* (ex. V, m. 53), *Taci, ohime* (ex. XVI, m. 47), and *Torna indietro* (ex. XXII, m. 44).

43. See *Pietà, spietati* (ex. XXI, m. 36), *Risolvetevi* (ex. XIII, m. 29), *Speranze, sentite* (ex. XIV, m. 14).

44. See *Lungi* (ex. XX, m. 50), *Mi contento* (ex. XVII, m. 12), *Non mi fate* (ex. XI, m. 20), *Respira* (ex. V, second ending, m. 63 and third ending, m. 61), *Torna indietro* (ex. XXII, m. 52).

45. See *E può* (ex. XV, m. 44), *Hor guardate*, (ex. IX, m. 15), *Non mi lusingar* (ex. XXIV, m. 70).

46. Most of the cantatas that open in this manner are solo cantatas. In the ensembles the motto-like introductory gesture appears infrequently. Longer imitative passages, or recitative for solo voice, are typical.

47. I use this term for the memorable melodic gesture at the close of Monteverdi's *Il Combattimento di Tancredi e Clorinda*. This melodic embellishment reappears thousands of times in Luigi's generation and the one following. Besides the examples indicated, see the incipits of *Tenti, Misero cor, Occhi soavi, Horche l'oscuro, Quando spiega* and *Adagio* in Thematic Index 1.

48. The same motto is used to introduce a unit in the arie di più parti *Furie d'averno* and *Credei col gir*, both listed in Thematic Index 2; these too are in the minor mode and the descending fourth is also diminished.

49. Burrows, *The Italian Cantata* I (Wellesley College, 1963), p. 80, measures 188-191. This stock motive, apparently a common one, opens the duo *Luci belle* (Thematic Index 2), the anonymous "morale" *Cangia sensi* (*I* MOe, M.G. 306), *Son contento di non amare* (*F* Pbn, Vm 7 4, anon), and the aria "Fidi amanti" in Provenzale's *Gionto il fatale dì* (Thematic Index 1) where it is repeated as in Cesti's paraphrase. A rhythmic variant of the motto begins the anonymous cantata *Bella cosa* (*I* Rvat, Barb. 4208).

50. Related to this form of contrast is the juxtaposition of the two segments of the tonic or the the dominant octave characteristic of the "All'armi" and "Sperate" migrating motives that occur primarily at the opening of a unit (see above, pp. 76-77). Contrast of this kind is a feature of a whole group of motto openings—*A chi, lasso, A i sospiri, Ho vinto, Luci belle, dite, ohime, Mai no'l dirò, Mi contento, Quanto è credulo* and the aria "Su, mio cor" from the cantata *Horche l'oscuro manto* as well as the anonymous cantatas *Ciglia brune* and *Il mio core chi l'ha* (Thematic Index 2) are among the cantatas that begin with tonic-dominant and octave contrasts.

51. The ternary cantatas *All'ombra, Amor, e perche* (ex. XII), and *Fanciulle, tenete* (in the last mentioned, the repetition occurs at the beginning of the second segment of the strophe); the rondos *Che sventura, La bella che mi contenta, Non la volete* and *Speranze, sentite*; the rounded binary *Ho perso* and binary cantatas *Apritevi* and *No, mio bene*, where the repetition occurs at the beginning of the second unit and was no doubt inspired by the text: "Raddoppiatemi le pene!"

52. Change of meter and tempo occurs after the introductory passage in the binary cantatas *Amanti, ardire, Ahi, dunque, Chiuda, Datemi pace, Di capo, Dolenti pensieri, Mai no'l dirò, Mani alteri, Mio core, Misero cor, Perche ratto, Precorrea, Sognai* and *Tenti*; the rondos *Amor giura, Che cosa, Chi può Deh, soffri, Libertà, ragion, Si, v'ingannate, Sospiri, su, su* and *Speranze, che dite*; the ternary cantata *Quando io credo* and the rounded binary *Non mi fate mentire*.

53. The envelope design is defined above, p. 33.

54. The binary cantatas *Com'è breve*, *Già finita*, *Guardate dove*, *Mai finirò*, *Non m'affligete*, *No, mio bene*, *O cieli* and *Taci, ohime*; the ternary *Amor, e perche*, *A te, mio core*, *Difenditi, o core*, *E d'amore* and *Non c'è che dire*; all the rounded binary cantatas except *Mio core*, *Quante volte* and *Rendetevi*; and the rondos *Che cosa*, *Ch'io speri*, *Chi può*, *Come penare*, *Così va*, *E chi non*, *E si crede*, *Hor guardate*, *Mi contento*, *Nessun*, *No, non ci pensa*, *Quanto è credulo*, *Si v'ingannate*, *Speranze, sentite* and also the refrains of the rondos of the arie di più parti *Da perfida*, *Giusto così*, *Non più viltà* and *S'era alquanto*.

55. This occurs in *Come penare*, *Così va*, *Da perfida*, *Difenditi, o core*, (ex. VII), *E chi non*, *Hor guardate* (ex. IX), *Già finita*, *Giusto così*, *Risolvetevi* (ex. XIII), *Speranze, sentite* (ex. XIV), *Su, su*, and *Taci, ohime* (ex. XVI).

56. Some examples are the envelope designs of *Begl'occhi, pietà*, *Che cosa* (ex. VIII), *Che vuoi*, *Ch'io speri*, *Nessun* and *No, non ci pensa*.

57. In *Uscite di porto* (ex. VI), where this procedure is also used, the segment of the introductory passage that is quoted first appears with the second verse—this is one of the cantatas whose introductory passage is the setting of two verses rather than one. However, in the envelope only the first verse is recapitulated.

58. Examples are the envelope designs of *Difenditi, amore* (ex. III), *Ho perso* and *Io non amo*.

59. Envelope designs of this type are in *Amor, e perche*, *A te*, *Disperati*, *E d'amore*, *E si crede*, *Guardate dove*, *Mai finirò*, *No, mio bene*, *O cieli*, *Quanto è credulo*, *Respira, core* and *S'era alquanto*.

60. This occurs even in the cantatas with a change of meter after the introductory passage (*Che cosa*, *Chi può*, *Mai no'l dirò*, *Non mi fate* and *Si v'ingannate*); with the return to the reprise verse there is a return to the original meter.

61. The binary cantata *Non m'affligete* (ex. XXV), where the opening and closing passages of the first unit are identical, is probably not Luigi's (see below, pp. 93-94). The da capo rubric at the close of the refrain of *Tu sarai* suggests a similar envelope design in which the entire (and long) opening passage is quoted intact before the second unit. This is entirely unusual and may be an error. See p. 100.

62. See ex. XXIII, the second unit of *Quando più*, which begins with four four-measure phrases, each the setting of an octosyllable; the four phrases that follow are of 15, four, seven, and eight measures respectively. Other examples are in the cantatas *A me stesso*, *Begl'occhi, pietà*, *Che sventura*, *Fate quel che volete*, *Hor guardate*, *La bella più bella*, *No, non ci pensa*, *Se dolente*, *Sospiri, olà*, *Sparite dal volto*.

63. Musico-poetic rhythmic patterns recur regularly forming the whole or the greater part of both units of *Adorate mie catene*, *Che dici, mio core*, *Ch'io speri*, *Deh soffri* (the pattern is broken several times in the first unit, but is maintained in the second), *Difendi, mio core*, *Difenditi, amore* (ex. III; here too the pattern is more strictly ad-

hered to in the second unit), *E si crede, Fanciulla son'io, Guardatevi, olà, Io lo vedo* (published in *HAM*), *Luci mie da me sparite, Speranze, che dite* (ex. XXVII), *Su, su, su, mio core*, and a single unit of *Mi contento* (third unit) and *Sento al cor* (second unit).

64. Putnam Aldrich, *Rhythm in Seventeenth-Century Italian Monody* (New York: W. W. Norton, 1966), pp. 114-133.

65. Ibid., p. 130.

66. Ibid.

67. Ibid., p. 131.

68. Ibid., p. 132.

69. By phrase in this discussion I mean a group of measures that makes complete sense as a separate unit ("sentence"); I do not mean the two- and three-measure units, also properly called phrases, that form segments of larger groups.

70. Only two consecutive phrases are equal in length—the six-measure phrases preceding the final phrases of the cantata—otherwise there are but two other phrases of the same length, the first (mm. 1-10) and the phrase beginning in measure 60 and extending through measure 69.

71. In those cases where sequence occurs with new words, the verses of the sequence and its model are invariably of the same number of syllables; see, for example, *Che cosa* (ex. VIII), the second unit, with the words "E spera ch'al core/per opra d'amore," mm. 33-35; *Difenditi, amore* (ex. III), the second unit, with "le voci, le strida/gl'affanni, i lamenti," mm. 26-28; *Difenditi, o core*, (ex. VII), mm. 3-4, 7-9, 21-23; *Non mi fate* (ex. XI), the beginning of the second unit; *Respira* (ex. V), the second unit, mm. 38-45; and *Speranze, che dite* (ex. XXVII), the third unit, mm. 94-99, 105-112.

72. See, for example, the second units of *Amor, e perche* (ex. XII), *Il contento* (ex. XIX), *Non mi lusingar* (ex. XXIV), *Speranze, che dite* (ex. XXVII), and *Speranze, sentite* (ex. XIV).

73. The prevalence of sequence in *Difenditi, o core* (ex. VII) is exceptional. Although not as predominant as in *Difenditi*, sequence is found in a greater degree than is normally typical in the cantata *Se dolente*.

74. In the shorter ariette there is somewhat less use of sequence; see *Amor, e perche* (ex. XII), *Che cosa* (ex. VIII), *Difenditi, amore* (ex. III), *Hor guardate* (ex. IX), *Non mi fate* (ex. XI), *Quando spiega* (ex. II) and *Respira* (ex. V).

75. Also see the opening of *M'uccidete* (ex. XVIII), the conclusion of *Taci, ohime* (ex. XVI, mm. 34-39, 40-45; the single alteration in the sequence occurs in measure 43 where F is left unembellished), the conclusion of the first unit of the aria di più parti *Horche l'oscuro* (recorded by Pleiades Records, P 103), and the close of the first unit

of *Lungi da me*; here, as mentioned earlier, the deviation makes the cadence a quotation at pitch.

76. For exact sequences see ex. VIII, second unit, with the repetition of "va, segui pur bellezza"; ex. XII, mm. 6-8; ex. XX, mm. 69-74, 81-85; ex. I, mm. 45-48; ex. XXVII, third unit, mm. 93-99 and 104-110 (here consecutive hexasyllables rather than a repeated verse are set sequentially); for inexact sequences see ex. IV, mm. 19-20; ex. I, mm. 40-43; ex. III, mm. 25-27; ex. XI, mm. 12-14, 18-20; ex. IV, mm. 11-13, 13-16; ex. XVI, mm. 1-4.

77. See also ex. XXIV, mm. 20-25; ex. XXVII, mm. 14-20.

78. The parody *Sotto l'ombra*, the longest of Luigi's cantatas (it extends 460 measures), is the only cantata composed entirely in recitative, except for a five-measure phrase.

79. *Io non amo* and *Non mi fate*. Elsewhere in the rounded binary cantatas recitative passages form parts of the first units of *Non mi fate* and *Armatevi di sdegno* and the whole of the first unit of *Disperati*.

80. Prolongation cadences are rare or do not occur at all in some of the long recitative cantatas such as *Rugge quasi leon* and *Sotto l'ombra*. In *Hor si versate*, an aria di più parti formed mostly of recitative, the only prolongation cadence is the last one, which concludes a movement in bel canto style.

81. Examples of this kind of prolongation are many. A few of the cantatas in which it occurs are *Acuto gelo*, *Al cenno*, *Adagio, speranze*, *Che sospiri*, *Chi desia*, *Chi può*, *E d'amore*, *Ho vinto*, *Ho perduto*, *Mentre sorge*, *Mostro*, *Non lo dite*, *No, mio bene*, *Piangea*, *Pietà*, *spietati*, *Poiche mancò*, *Quanto è credulo*, *Questo piccol*, *Respira*, *Rendetevi*, *Se mai ti punge*, *Soffrirei*, *Tu sarai*, *Voi sete*.

82. The fact that most of the examples here and below are in the key of E minor does not mean that such cadences occur only in this key, but points to the predominance of cantatas in E minor. Among the examples cited in the footnotes on this page and the next are cadences in the keys of C minor, D minor, A minor, G minor, F minor, B-flat major, and D major.

83. Examples of the second type of prolongation are found in *Che pretendete*, *E chi non*, *Horche l'oscuro*, *Io ero*, *Lo splendor*, *No, mio bene*, *O cieli*, *Perche ratto*, *Poiche mancò*, *Precorrea*, *Rendetevi*, *Sempre dunque*, *Sparite dal volto*, *Speranze, sentite*, *Spiega un volo*, *Tra romite*, *Tu giuri*, *Un cor*, *Un pensiero*, *Un tiranno*, *Voi sete troppo*.

84. Examples of the third type occur in *Che farò*, *E può soffrirsi*, *Fingi*, *Horche l'oscuro*, *Horche notte* (where the two other kinds are also present), *O dura*, *Se mi volete*, *Sospiri miei*, *Torna indietro*, *Tenti e ardisca*.

85. See also *No, mio bene*, ex. 28a, above, where a prolongation of the second type is followed by a prolongation phrase of the first type.

86. At the close of the first unit of *Ho vinto* the abrupt change from F major to F minor coincides with the words "mortal sembianza"; in *Come tosto* the words "giovinezza

mortale" are set with a juxtaposition of A and A-flat in a cadence to F. With the cry "ahi, che mi morirò!" in *Fanciulla son'io*, a D-flat suddenly appears in the context of B-flat major. Within the rondo refrain of *Che sventura* there is a sudden movement from C major to C minor with the exclamation "che languisco, che mi moro!"

87. In the binary cantata *Amor s'io mi querelo* short ritornelli are interjected within the second unit separating the first from the second phrase and the second from the last. This kind of articulation within a unit of any type of cantata is rare.

88. *Adorate, Amor così, Che dici, Che vuoi, Da perfida, E d'amore, Piangea, Quando più, S'era alquanto, Sparsa il crine, Spenti gl'affanni, Speranze al tuo.*

89. A ritornello occurs in three ternary, three rounded binary, eight binary, 24 rondo cantatas, four laments and 23 arie di più parti. It appears much less frequently in Luigi's cantatas than in the cantatas of his younger contemporaries. There is hardly a cantata by Carlo Caproli, for example, in which there is no ritornello.

90. In four binary cantatas the ritornello concludes both units; in two, it concludes the first only; and in two others, the second only.

91. When the ritornello cadence does recur at the close of a cantata there may be a reason that makes its presence necessary. For example, at the end of the rounded binary *Olà, pensieri*, the recurrence of the ritornello from the first unit seems essential, for without it the cantata would end without a perfect cadence.

92. The exceptional cantata is *E d'amore*; see p. 121, note 27.

93. The limitation of the meaning of the term to "reiterated cadence" is evident in the *Concerts Royaux* by François Couperin (Paris, Durand & Fils, n.d.). In these instrumental suites each movement closes with cadences formed of its own particular thematic material without quoting from any other movement. Usually the final cadence of each movement is repeated; it is the repeated cadence that sometimes bears the designation "ritornello." Hence "ritornello" does not necessarily mean "recurring," except in a very special and limited sense.

94. In the repertory of the mid-century cantata, examples of ritornelli whose upper parts are written out are rare. The few that I have seen are in Luigi's *Al cenno, Giusto cosi* and *Guardatevi, olà* and in the anonymous cantatas *Filli, un cielo* (Nc. 33.4.7) and *Come sarebbe a dire* (*I* Pc. CF-III-1).

95. The ritornello at the close of *Al cenno* is notated only in one of the MS sources containing this cantata, the MS *F* Pa, M. 99.

96. Concerning the ciaccona and passacaglia bass formulae see Thomas Walker, "Ciaccona and Passacaglia: Remarks on Their Origin and Early History," *JAMS* XXI (1968), 300-320, and Richard Hudson, "The Passacaglia and Ciaccona in Italian Keyboard Music of the 17th Century," *The Diapason*; Nov. and Dec. 1969, 10-11 and 6-7. As far as I have determined, the *Al cenno* ritornello is the only example of a ciaccona soggetto in Luigi's cantatas either as a ritornello or as the repeated motive of an ostinato segment.

97. In the MS *I* Nc, 33.4.7, at the close of the reprise of the ternary cantata *Filli, un cielo*. The rubric also occurs in the MS *I* Nc, 33.4.12 in Provenzale's aria di più parti *Gionto il fatale dì* between the strophes of the binary arietta "Fidi amanti."

98. In the MS *I* Bc, Q 47 with each of the three appearances of a typical ritornello bass in the duet *Chi fa che ritorni* from Marazzoli's *La Vita Humana*, Act II.

99. In the MS *B* Bc, Litt. F 695 between two units of the anonymous cantata *Ferma, o tempo*.

100. In the MS *I* Rc, 2472 (here the ritornello is not attached to any cantata but is notated on the last page of the MS) and in the MS *GB* Och, 998 at the close of a strophe towards the end of Caproli's aria di più parti *Non si tema*. The "Passag(aglio)" is almost identical to the ritornello at the close of the preceding strophe marked "ritornello" (Ex. 34); each is in the key of the strophe it concludes.

101. Hudson, "Passacaglia and Ciaccona," p. 11.

102. Ibid., formula N3.

103. The ten cantatas are the rondos *A chi, lasso*, *Che dici*, *Chi trovasse*, *Come penare*, *E chi non v'ameria*, *Quando meco*; the lament *Pender*, and the arie di più parti *Dove più giro*, *Fingi* and *Torna indietro*.

104. The cadence is heard twice in each of the binary cantatas *Addio, perfida*, *Al bel lume*, *Amanti, ardire*, *Dissi ad amore*, *Mio core, di che* and *Speranza, al tuo*; it is the final cadence of one of the units of the binary *Al far del dì*, *Lungi da me*, *Occhi quei vaghi* and *O cieli*. In the ternary cantata *Mortale, che pensi* it is the penultimate cadence; in the rounded binary *Non mi lusingar* it concludes the introductory segment of the first unit, and in *Uscite di porto* it concludes the third strophe. The cadence also concludes three units of the aria di più parti *Spiega un volo* and the first and last trios of *Horche in notturno*. It is found with melodic and rhythmic variants at the close of the arie di più parti *Mostro*, *Quando mi chiede* and *Sparite dal volto*. It is the penultimate cadence of *Chi non sa* and concludes the octosyllablic aria of *Anime*, both arie di più parti.

105. In *Anime* and *Quando mi chiede* the cadence is found in duple meter. The only version in the major mode that I know is in *Occhi quei vaghi*.

106. This theme also occurs in Luigi's *Begl'occhi, che dite*, *Che dici, mio core*, *Disperati*, *Sospiri, su, su* and *Uscite di porto*; in the anonymous cantatas *Bambino divino*, F Pth, H.P. 29; *Vi par pur poco*, D MUs, 4087; *Sentite come fu*, *I* Pc, CF 111-I; *Che dite, pensieri, d'un fiero volto*, F Pbn, Vm 7 4; *Begl'occhi, e che sarà*, F Pth, H.P. 31; *Begl'occhi, tiranni*, (see Thematic Index 2); in Caproli's *Giurai cangiar pensiero*, *I* Rc, 2483; in Tenaglia's *Begl'occhi, scoccate*, *I* Rvat, Chigi *Q* IV 18, and *Non voglio*, *I* Nc, 33.4.15, I; Carissimi's *Lungi da me*, see *WECIS*, 5; Savioni's *Begl'occhi, mirate* and *Son morto*, see *WECIS*, 2, and Marciani's *Mio core, mio bene*, (see Thematic Index, 2).

107. This variant is also found in Caproli's *Giurai cangiar pensiero*, Tenaglia's *Non voglio* and *Begl'occhi, scoccate*, and in the anonymous *Begl'occhi, e che sarà*.

108. This also occurs in the anonymous arietta *Sentite come fu*.

109. This also occurs in the second and third measures of *Che dici*, and at the opening of the second unit of *Disperati* (ex. IV). A related version is the close of the opening phrase of *Begl'occhi, che dite*, where the theme is extended.

110. The "Adorate" theme also appears in Luigi's *A la rota, Di capo ad Amarilli, E che cantar, Gelosia, Giusto così, Mi contento, Mortale, che pensi, Quando meco, Soffrirei, Sparite dal core, Spiega un volo*; in Marc'Antonio Pasqualini's *Non mi lusingar* and in the anonymous cantatas *Dentro negra foresta*, Thematic Index 2; *Non mi turbate, I* Rvat, 4208; *Poiche al lido*, Thematic Index 2.

111. These six-syllable verses are all of the kind in which the last syllable is accented; in Italian poetry such a verse is called "settenario tronco"—it is considered a heptasyllable.

112. The binary cantatas *A i sospiri, A qual dardo, Chi mi credeva, Chiuda quest'occhi, De la vita, Dopo lungo, Due feroci, Filli, non penso, Gelosia, Già nel oblio, Hor ch'avvolte, Hor ch'io, Il cor mi dice, Ingordo human, Io che sin, Luci belle, Perche ratto, Poiche mancò, Quando spiega, Quasi baleno, Questo piccol* and *Tenti*; the rondos *Che dici, Che pretendete, Chi non ha, Chi può, Con voi parlo, Fanciulla son'io, La bella che mi, La bella più bella, Luci mie, Mai finirò, Quanto è credulo, Sento al cor* (strophic variations also occur in the rondos of the arie di più parti *Giusto così, Sopra conca* and *V'è, v'è*), and the rounded binary *Uscite di porto*.

113. A striking exception is *Fanciulla son'io*. In the version given in most of the MSS sources, the refrain is varied and the second unit is not. In the MS *GB* Och, 17 both units are varied and the variations of the first unit are unlike those in the other MSS.

114. This is true of the refrain of *Fanciulla son'io* and the second units of *La bella più bella, Con voi, Luci mie, Mai finirò* and *Sento al cor* (also the second units of the rondos in the arie di più parti *Sopra conca* and *V'è, v'è*).

115. *Chiuda quest'occhi, Gelosia, Già nel oblio, Hor ch'io, Ingordo human, Io che sin, Luci belle, Precorrea, Quando spiega*, and *Questo piccol*.

116. The arie di più parti *A la rota, Da perfida, E che pensi, Horche fra l'ombre, Horch'in notturna, Horche l'oscuro, Horche notte, Lo splendor, Mentre sorge, Mostro, Noi siam, Ombre fuggite, Pria ch'al sdegno, Se non corre, Sopra conca, Tutto cinto, V'è, v'è*; the laments *Erminia, Hora ch'ad eclissar, Pender*; the binary *Ahi, dunque, Deggio, De la vita, Dopo lungo, E può soffrirsi, Guardate dove, Ho perduto, Occhi belli, occhi miei, Tenti*; the rondos *A chi, lasso, Che dici, Con voi, Fanciulla son'io, La bella per cui, La bella più bella, Luci mie, Mai finirò, Sento al cor, Sulla veglia*; the rounded binary *Disperati, Io non amo, M'uccidete, Rendetevi, Respira*; the ternary *Fanciulle, tenete* and *Quando più mia libertà*.

117. The exceptions are the strict ostinato, *La bella più bella, Che dici*, where the technique encompasses both the whole of the refrain and all but the last segment of the second unit, and *La bella per cui*, where the ostinato is a brief passage within the second unit that comments on the lover's foolhardiness.

118. The descending chromatic tetrachord appears in only one other arietta corta, the binary *Ho perduto* (ex. 81) mentioned above, p. 84.

119. The one other example of text ostinato that I have found in Luigi's cantatas is in the duo *Spiega un volo*, an aria di più parti. The affective repetition of "ohime, ohime!" is heard in the central part of the cantata, the second section that is formed by two quatrains instead of one as are the sections on either side of it.

120. When it embellishes the concluding phrase of a unit, the melisma is usually placed on the fourth or fifth last syllable, whichever is accented.

121. Barton Hudson, "Notes on Gregorio Strozzi and his Capricci," *JAMS* XX (Summer 1967), p. 212.

122. Such variants are found in the different versions of the cantatas *A la rota, Chi batte, Difenditi, amore, Gelosia* (see below, pp. 92-93), *Horche in notturna* and *Horche l'oscuro*. Not only are melismatic passages altered in *Chiuda quest'occhi, Cor dolente* and *Fanciulla son io*, but the cantatas as a whole undergo considerable revision. (The different versions of *Cor dolente* are briefly described below, p. 131, note 15.)

Notes for Chapter 3

1. Normally the shortest segment in the binary cantatas is the first segment of the second unit. Only in three cantatas, *Ahi, dunque, No, mio bene* and *Ho perduto*, is this segment longer than the conclusion, and uniquely in *Occhi belli* it is longer than the first unit.

2. This procedure is also used in the concluding segments of *Addio, perfida, A tanti sospiri, Occhi quei vaghi* and *Se dolente*.

3. Examples of recurring cadences are found in the binary cantatas *Addio, perfida, Al bel lume, Amanti, ardire, Amor se devo, Che sospiri, E può soffrirsi, Ha cent'occhi, Mio cor di che, No, mio bene, Non m'affligete, Questo piccol, Sognai, Son divenuto, Spenti, Speranza al tuo*; in the rondos *Deh, soffri, Se non corre, Si v'ingannate, Tu sarai*; the ternary cantata *Soffrirei* and the arie di più parti *Fingi, Horche l'oscuro, Sospiri miei, Spiega un volo*, and *Torna indietro*.

4. The binary design occurs quite often within the arie di più parti and forms a single unit.

5. Charles Parry, *The Oxford History of Music* (Oxford, 1902), III, 153 ff., and Henri Prunières, "La cantate italienne à voix seule au dix-septième siècle," *Encyclopédie de la Musique* (1913), II, 5, p. 3406.

6. *Gelosia* is published in Gv, I, 39 ff. (see Volume 2, Musical Sources).

7. As previously noted, this is not in keeping with Luigi's usual practice, which is to keep the music of a refrain intact.

8. The recurrence of an entire phrase with new text in a subsequent section of a cantata has some precedence in Luigi's arie di più parti (*Lasciatemi qui solo*, *Pria ch'al sdegno*, *Ravvolse* and *Sospiri miei*), but not in the ariette corte.

9. *Io piangea*, *Mi danno la morte* and *Se mai ti punge*. Besides the last-mentioned cantata, the chord of the lowered second degree is heard only in one other binary piece, *Un tiranno*. Among the other ariette corte, it is found in the rondo *Mi contento* and the rounded binary *Sei pur dolce*. The "Neapolitan Sixth" occurs relatively more frequently in the arie di più parti, but usually no more than once in any cantata: *Filli, un cielo*, *Io piangea*, *Lasciatemi qui solo*, *Lasciate ch'io ritorni*, *Lascia speranza*, *Lo splendor*, *Horche in notturna* (the trio "Dormite"), *Mi danno*, *Non m'asciugate*, *O dura*, *Patienza*, *Perche speranze*, *Rugge*, *Sospiri miei*, *Sotto l'ombra*, *V'è, v'è*.

10. *Ferma, Giove*, *Non più viltà*, *Se mi volete* and *Se non corre*.

11. *Da perfida*, *Giusto così*, *Ombre fuggite*, *S'era alquanto*, *Sopra conca* and *V'è, v'è*.

12. *Adorate*, *Che dici*, *Che farò*, *Ch'io speri* and *Speranze, che dite*.

13. The rondos *Che farò*, *Che sventura*, *Come penare*, *Così va*, *Fate quel*, *Hor guardate*, *Libertà*, *Mi contento* (fourth unit), *Ne notte*, *Nessun*, *Si v'ingannate*, *Speranze, sentite*. The ternary *All'ombra*, *Amor, e perche*, *E d'amore*, *Fanciulle, tenete*, *Non c'è che dire*. Of the arie di più parti that contain a rondo or that are extended rondos, two-part units are found in *Da perfida*, *Ferma, Giove*, *Giusto così*, *Ombre fuggite*, *Se non corre* and *Sopra conca*.

14. The second and third units of *Sospiri, su, su*, whose text is like that of *Speranze, sentite*, are so similar that the third is almost a strophic repetition of the first. The two units share all but two phrases; the close of the second unit borrowed from the refrain is not heard in the third unit, and one passage in the third unit is not present in the second.

15. Oddly enough, it is in the ternary version that the settings of the first unit differ; in the rondo version, given uniquely in *I* Bc, Q 48, the first unit returns without change as a rondo refrain—the MS gives a second stanza for the strophic repetition of the second unit. In the other sources the first unit is extended in its single recapitulation by the addition of an inner phrase of five measures, and by three measures added to the beginning of the last phrase. In addition, the original trio setting is expanded to four voices. The credibility of the rondo version is not enhanced by the carelessness of its notation in MS Q 48. The second unit is marked by neglect of rhythmic details, by the omission of a melismatic passage, and by unverifiable changes in the melodic line.

16. *Amor giura*, *Che dici*, *Con amor*, *Come penare*, *Difendi, mio core*, *Fanciulla son'io*, *Guardatevi, olà*, *Ferma Giove*, *La bella più bella*, *Luci mie*, *No, non ci pensa*, *Non più viltà*, *Quanto è credulo*, *Se mi volete*, *S'era alquanto*, *Sospiri, su, su*.

17. *No, non ci pensa*, *Quanto è credulo*, *Sospiri, su, su* and the arie di più parti *Non più viltà* and *S'era alquanto*. The final statement of the refrain in the rondo unit of *S'era alquanto* is a recapitulation of the first only in the MS *I* Rvat, Barb. 4207; in the other

sources the rondo unit closes with a single phrase derived from the conclusion of the original refrain setting. If this cantata is indeed by Luigi, it is surely a late work; its style is very similar to Caproli's and it would not be surprising if it should turn up in another MS attributed to Caproli. *I* Rvat, 4207, one of the sources in which it is anonymous, contains cantatas of Cesti's and Caproli's generation. Of its contents—all of which are anonymous except for a cantata attributed to "Sig. Antonio Cesti"—six are attributed to Cesti and five to Caproli in other sources. No cantata other than *S'era alquanto* is attributed to Rossi elsewhere. *GB* Cfm, 24.F.4, the one source that attributes the cantata to Luigi, is unreliable in several of its attributions. It is likely that the copy of *S'era alquanto* in this MS was made from the MSS Harley 1264 and 1863 where the cantata is anonymous.

18. In the rondos composed by the generation after Luigi, alterations such as are exemplified in *Quanto è credulo* are much more common than are symmetrical and exact repetitions of the rondo refrain.

19. The text of this cantata is discussed above, p. 46.

20. This procedure is also found in Marco Marazzoli's *Hai raigon tu* (*I* Rvat, Chigi Q VIII 177).

21. The systematic adoption of the ternary scheme A b A in numerous arias is not one of Luigi's contributions, contrary to what has been stated (Abbiati, *Storia della Musica* (Milano: Garzanti, 1946), II, p. 316), unless one includes within the definition of the ternary form the rondo extension of the ternary principle.

22. *I* Rc, 2478, ff. 60-69v, and *I* Rvat, Barb. 4223, ff. 106-109v.

23. *Armatevi di sdegno, Che vuoi, Quante volte* and *Risolvetevi*.

24. *Disperati, Non mi fate, Rendetevi, Sei pur dolce* and *Su, su, mio core*. *Rendetevi* is formed like *Quante volte*—without the second statement of the reprise verse in the first unit: A b // c A' //.

25. *Begl'occhi, pietà, Difenditi, amore, Ho perso, Io non amo, M'uccidete, Ohime, madre, Olà, pensieri, Respira, Uscite di porto*. *Mio core languisce* also belongs to this group of strophic cantatas although its first section is composed somewhat differently; see below, p. 107. The text of the second stanza of the second unit of *Ho perso* is unique in that it retains not only the concluding reprise, but also the quatrain of hexasyllables that precedes it in the first stanza. The second unit, thus, is composed of three segments: the initial seven hexasyllables, the quatrain retained in the second stanza, and the closing reprise. *Ho perso* is also the only cantata in which the concluding segment recalls not only the last verse of the opening unit, but the penultimate as well.

26. *Begl'occhi, Che vuoi, Difenditi, Disperati, Ho perso, Io non amo, Mio core, M'uccidete, Ohime, Olà, pensieri, Respira, Risolvetevi* and *Su, su*.

27. The version published by Riemann is a different one.

28. *Armatevi di sdegno, Non mi fate mentire, Sei pur dolce* and *Uscite*.

29. The second text is given only in the source of the anonymous solo version.

30. Quite different is the procedure in the anonymous solo version. There is no musical reprise, only text recurrence. The recurring verse has three different musical settings. This is a rare procedure. (Something of the same order takes place in Luigi's binary piece *Mai no'l dirò*.)

Example 1.

Tutto cinto di ferro

Example 2.

Correa l'ottavo giorno

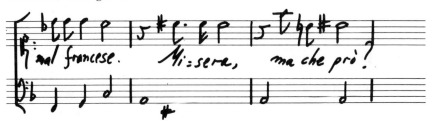

Example 3.

Con amor si pugna invano

Example 4.
Begl'occhi, pietà, first unit
a) Introductory passage

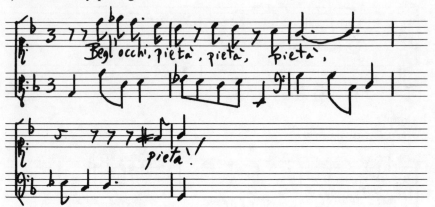

b) Concluding passage:

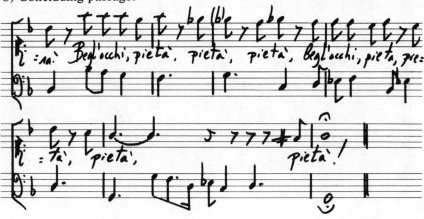

Example 5.
Sei pur dolce, o libertà, first unit
a) Introductory passage:

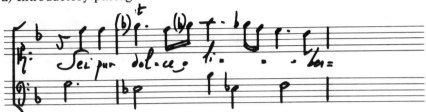

b) Concluding passage:

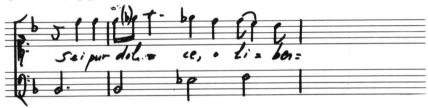

c) The continuation of both:

Example 6.

Olà, pensieri, olà, first unit

a) Introductory passage:

b) Concluding passage:

Example 7.
Apritevi, o begl'occhi

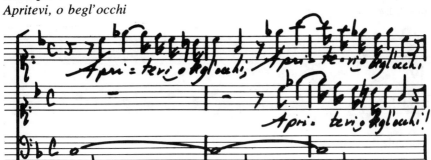

Example 8.
Sognai, lasso, sognai

Example 9.
Querelatevi di me se vi miro

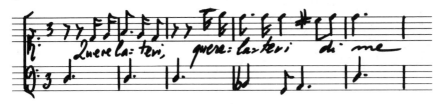

Example 10.
Amanti, ardire o goder

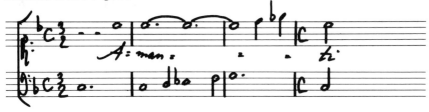

Example 11.
Aspettate! Adesso canto

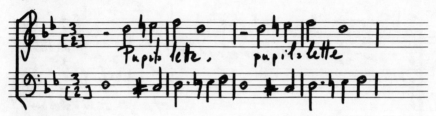

Example 12.
Ingordo human desio
a)

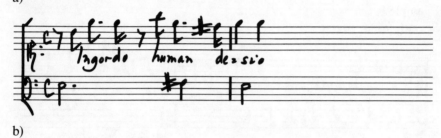

b)

c)

Example 13.
Perche ratto cosi
a)

b)

Example 14.
Al far del di

Example 15.
Ho perduto la fortuna

Example 16.
Ho perso il mio core

Example 17.
Armatevi di sdegno, offesi amanti, the first unit
a) Introductory passage:

b) Concluding passage:

Example 18.

Ohimè, madre, aita, aita, first unit

a) Introductory

b) Concluding passage:

Example 19.
Lungi da me, mio bene

a)

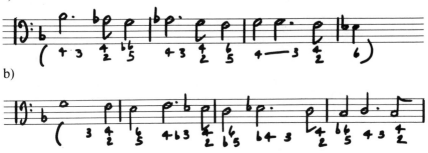

b)

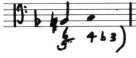

Example 20.
Fate quel che volete

Example 21.

Com' è breve il gioir

a)

b)

Example 22.

Ne notte ne dì

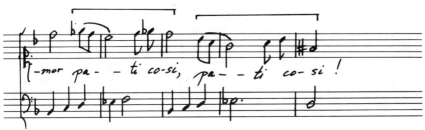

Example 23.

Se dolente e flebil cetra

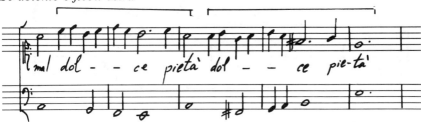

Example 24.

Soffrirei con lieto core

Example 25.
Perche ratto così

Example 26.
Questo piccol rio

Example 27.
Son divenuto amante
a)

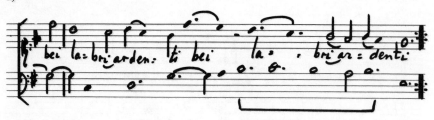

b)

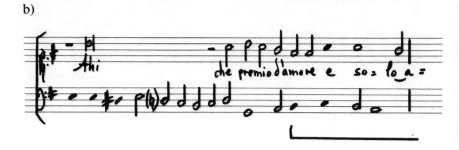

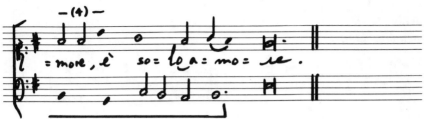

Example 28.
No, mio bene, non lo dite
a)

b)

Example 29.

Sempre, dunque, negarete

Example 30.
Ferma, Giove, ferma, conclusion of the refrain

Example 31.
Al cenno d'una speranza

Example 32.
Filli, un cielo è tua beltà
Passacaglio

Example 33.
Passagaglio

Example 34.
Non si tema
ritornello

passag·

Example 35.
a) *Adorate mie catene*

b) *E si crede ch'io no sò*

c) *Fanciulle, tenete il guard' a voi*

d) *Giusto così và detto*

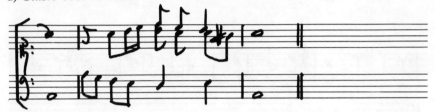

e) *Mai no'l dirò chi sia*

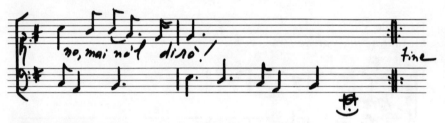

Example 36.
a) *Se non corre una speranza*

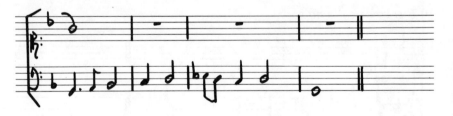

b) *Se mi volete morto*

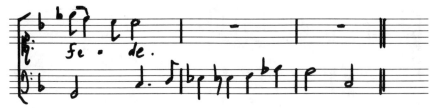

Example 37.
Quando meco tornerai

Example 38.
Speranza al tuo pallore
a) Close of the first unit:

b) Close of the second unit:

Example 39.
Amanti, ardire o goder
a) Close of the first unit:

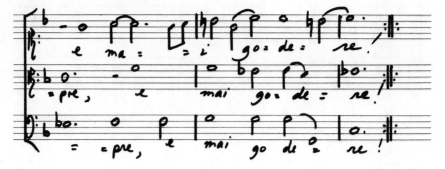

b) Close of the second unit:

Example 40.
O cieli, pietà, è l'alma svanita

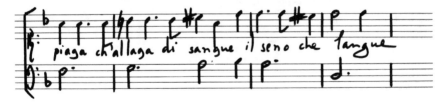

Example 41.
Dissi un giorno ad amore

Example 42.
Addio, perfida, addio
a) Close of the first unit:

b) Close of the second unit:

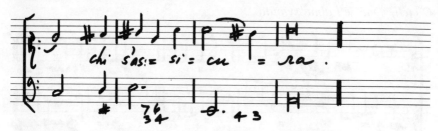

Example 43.
Occhi, quei vaghi azuri

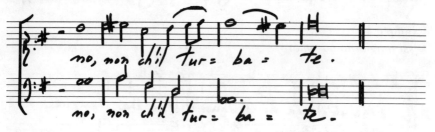

Example 44.

Al bel lume d'un bel volto

a) Close of the first unit:

b) Close of the second unit:

Example 45.
All'armi, mio core from *Orfeo*

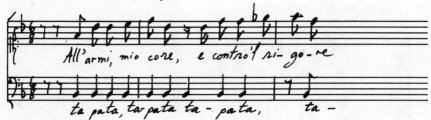

Example 46.
Nessun sene vanti di viver

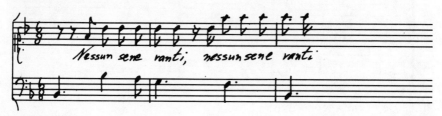

Example 47.
Se non corre una speranza

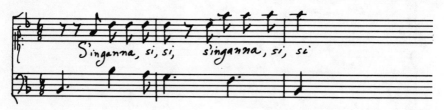

Example 48.
Occhi soavi, ogn'aspro cor

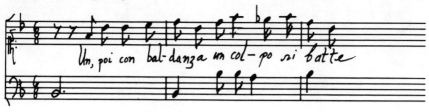

Example 49.
Difendi, mio core, l'entrata

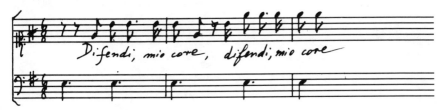

Example 50.
Sperate, o voi che avete
(*I* MOe, F 1265, Carlo Caproli)

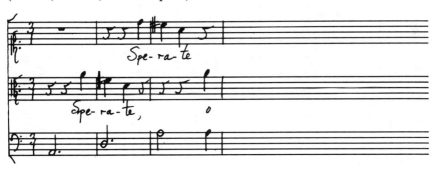

Example 51.
Mi contento così

Example 52.
Speranze, sentite

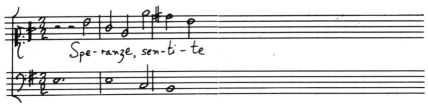

Example 53.
M'uccidete, begl' ecchi

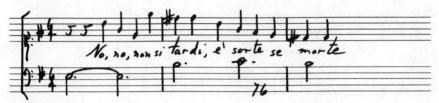

Example 54.
Herche notte guerriera

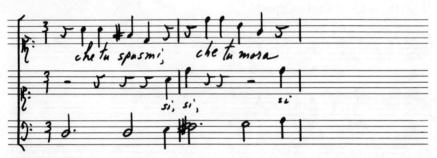

Example 55.
S'io son vinto, occhi belli

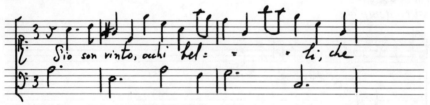

Example 56.
Ne notte, ne dì riposa quest'alma

Example 57.
Mortale, che pensi

a)

b)

c)

Example 58.
Adorate mie catene

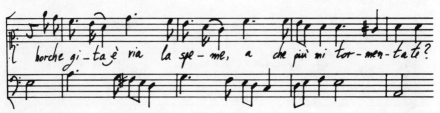

horche gi-ta è via la spe — me, a che più mi tor-men-ta te?

Example 59.
Che sventura! Son tant'anni

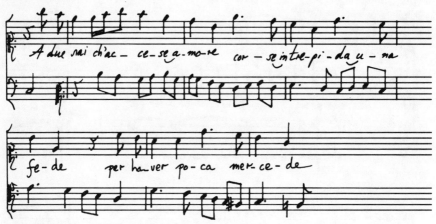

A due sai ch'ac — ce-se a-mo-re cor — se in tre-pi-da u — na

fe-de per ha ver po-ca mer-ce-de

Example 60.
Olà, pensieri, olà

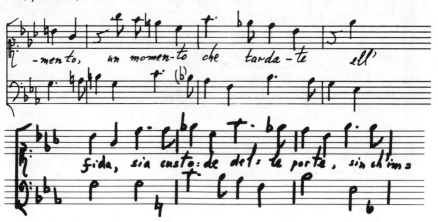

-men to, un momen-to che tarda-te ell'

fi da, sia custo:de del:la por ta, sin ch'im=

Example 61.
Non c'è che dire

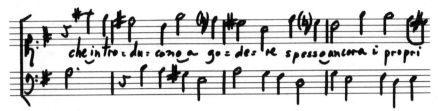

Example 62.
Lo splendor di due begl'occhi

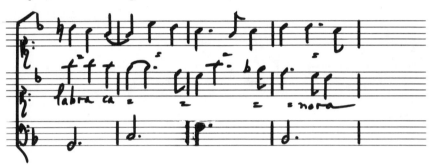

Example 63.
Perche chieder com'io sto

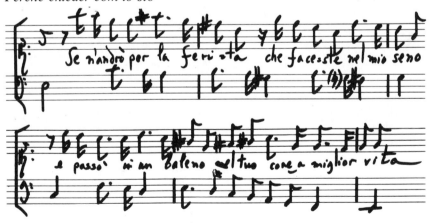

Example 64.
Sento al cor un non so che
a)

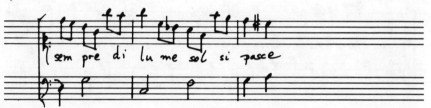

b)

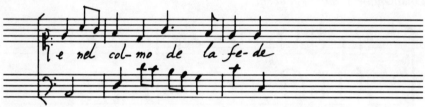

Example 65.
Perche ratto così
a) First and second strophes:

b) Third strophe:

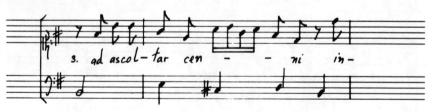

Example 66.
Vola, vola in altri petti, Alessandro Stradella

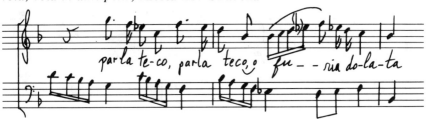

Example 67.
A tanti sospiri, a lagrime tante

Example 68.
S'io son vinto, occhi belli

Example 69.
Tenti e ardisca in amore

Example 70.
Cor dolente, ferito, schernito
a)

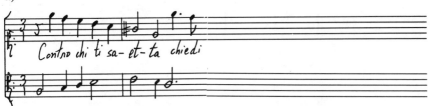

Contro chi ti sa- et- ta chiedi

b)

Contro chi ti sa- et- ta

Example 71.
Hor ch'io vivo lontano
a)

do - lor   re- ro   il ddor re - - - no.

b)

ri - gido il ver -   -   -   - no.

Example 72.

a) *Disperati*, *M'uccidete* and *Respira, core*

b) *Deggio dunque morire*

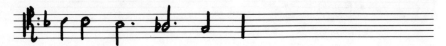

c) *La bella per cui son cieco*

d) *Occhi, belli, occhi miei*

e) *Rendetevi, pensieri*

f) *De la vita* and *Tenti e ardisca*

g) *Dopo lungo penare*

h) *Fanciulla son'io*

i) *Guardate dove và*

j) *Quando più mia libertà*

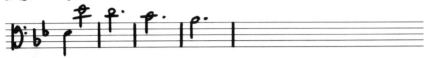

Example 73.
Luci mie, da me sparite

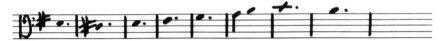

Example 74.
Con voi parlo, amanti

Example 75.
Mai finirò d'amare

Example 76.
Sento al cor un non so che

Example 77.
V'è, v'è che miro

Example 78.
A chi, lasso, crederò
a) Vm7 6

b) 4718a; Och, 17 and 350

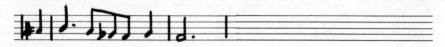

Example 79.
Ahi, dunque, è pur vero

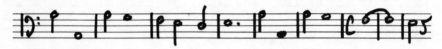

Example 80.
E può soffrirsi

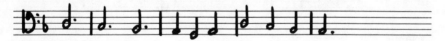

Example 81.
Ho perduto la fortuna

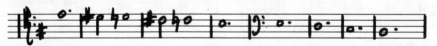

Example 82.
Io non amo, si

Example 83.
La bella più bella che il cor

Example 84.
Fanciulle, tenete il guardo

Example 85.
Sulla veglia d'una speme

Example 86.
Ingordo human desio

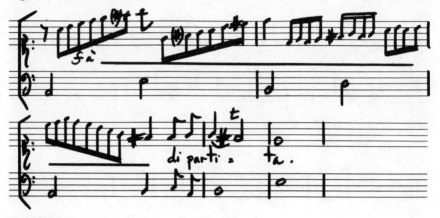

Example 87.
Gelosia ch'a poco a poco

Example 88.
E che cantar poss'io

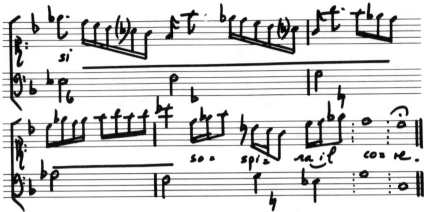

Example 89.
Sparite dal volto, loquaci pallori

Example 90.
Ahi, dunque, è pur vero

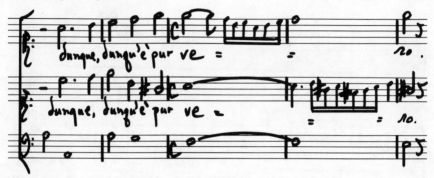

Example 91.
Gelosia ch'a poco a poco

Example 92.
Difendi, mio core

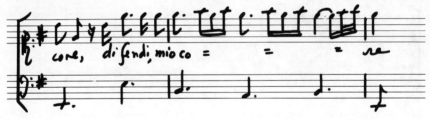

Example 93.
Questo piccol rio
a)

b)

Example 94.
Amor, se devo piangere

Example 95.
Filli, non penso più a destarti

Example 96.
Lasso, benche mi fugga

Example 97.
Sempre, dunque, negarete

Example 98.
Cum pervenisset Lucia
anonymous

Example 99.
Ferma, Giove, ferma, the closing arietta
a) Close of the first unit:

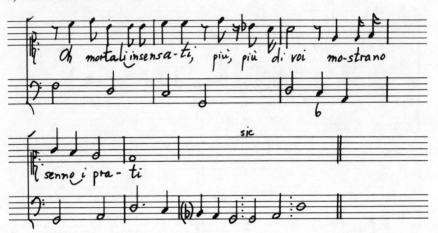

b) Close of the second unit:

Example 100.

Gelosia

a) Final phrase in MS Barb. lat. 4175:

b) Final phrase in MS de Bellis:

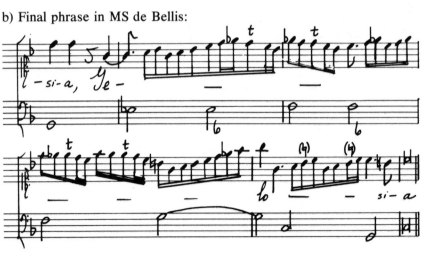

Example 101.
Sei pur dolce, e libertá, close of the second unit:

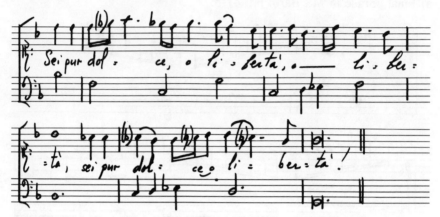

Example 102.
Armatevi di sdegno, offesi amanti, close of the second unit:

Example 103.
Rendetevi, pensieri
a)

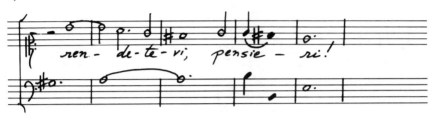

ren - de - te - vi, pensie - ri!

b)

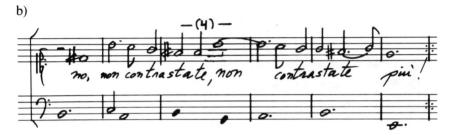

no, non contrastate, non contrastate più!

c)

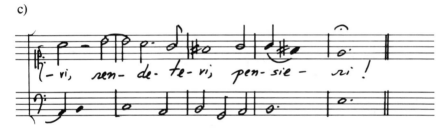

- vi, ren - de - te - vi, pen - sie - ri!

Example 104.
Quante volte l'ho dette

a)

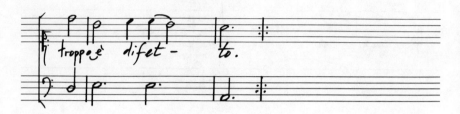

troppe è difet - to.

b)

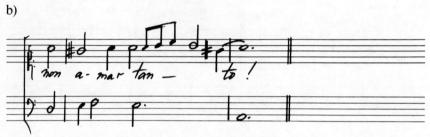

non a- mar tan — to!

c)

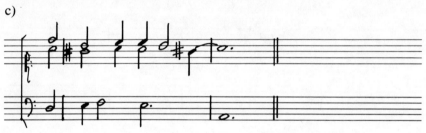

Tables of Cantatas

The Cantatas Attributed to Luigi Rossi on Reliable Grounds Alphabetically Listed

Page numbers are indicated for those discussed in Volume 1.

Con occhi belli (lament)
Con voi parlo (rondo), 80, 100
Cor dolente (rondo and ternary), 51, 78, 79, 99, 101, 169
Corilla danzando (binary)
Cosí va (rondo)

Da perfida speranza (aria di piú parti), 51, 94
Datemi pace (binary)
Deggio dunque (binary with closing refrain), 82, 83
Deh, perche (binary)
Deh, soccorri (rondo), 64
Deh, soffri (rondo), 100
De la vita (binary with closing refrain), 82, 85
Di capo ad Amarilli (binary)
Di desire (binary)
Difendi, mio core (rondo), 76, 87, 161, 176
Difenditi, amore (rounded binary), 5, 33, 35, 36, 41, 51, 76, 107, 111,
    112
Difenditi, o core (ternary), 33, 35, 36, 51, 105
Disperate speranze (ternary), 103
Disperati, che aspetti (rounded binary), 51, 82, 106
Dissi un giorno (binary), 157
Dite, o cieli (binary)
Diva, tu che in trono (binary)
Dolenti pensieri (binary with closing refrain)
Dopo lungo (binary), 82, 83
Dove, dove piú giro (aria di piú parti)
Due feroci guerrieri (binary), 39
Due labbra (binary), 39
D'una bella (binary)

E che cantar poss'io (aria di piú parti), 87, 175
E che pensi (aria di piú parti)
E chi non v'ameria (rondo)
E d'amore (ternary), 51, 64, 121, 127
E può soffrirsi (binary), 57, 67, 72, 82, 83
Erminia sventurata (lament)
E si crede (rondo), 46, 153

Fan battaglia (binary), 94, 127, 129
Fanciulla son'io (rondo), 37, 38, 51, 83, 154
Fanciulle, tenete (ternary), 84, 102, 103

Fate quel che volete (rondo), 33, 67, 145
Ferma, Giove (rondo-aria di piú parti), 73, 92, 95, 151, 180
Fillide mia (aria di piú parti)
Filli, non penso (binary with closing refrain), 87, 88, 178
Fingi ch'io t'ho tradito (aria di piú parti)
Frena il pianto (binary with closing refrain)

Già finita e per me (binary with closing refrain)
Già nel oblio (binary)
Giusto cosí va detto (aria di piú parti), 94, 127, 154
Guardate dove va (binary), 82, 83
Guardatevi, olà (rondo)

Ha cent'occhi (binary), 90
Ho perduto la fortuna (binary with closing refrain), 51, 82, 84, 130, 141
Ho perso il mio core (rounded binary), 60, 123, 132, 142
Hora ch'ad ecclissar (lament)
Horch'avvolte (binary)
Horche di marte (binary), 40
Horche fra l'ombra (aria di piú parti)
Horche in notturna pace (aria di piú parti)
Horche la notte del silentio
Horche l'oscuro (aria di piú parti)
Horche notte guerriera (aria di piú parti), 77, 162
Horch'io vivo (binary), 80, 169
Hor guardate (rondo), 51, 69, 74, 97, 105
Hor si, versate (aria di piú parti), 126
Ho vinto, gridava (binary), 126
Ho voto di non amare

Il contento (ternary), 65
Il cor mi dice (binary), 122
Infelici pensieri (aria di piú parti)
Ingordo human desio (binary with closing refrain), 61, 87, 140, 174
In questo duro (binary)
In solitario speco (lament), 20
Invan mi tendete (binary)
Io che sin hor (binary), 122
Io ero pargoletta (binary), 46
Io lo vedo (rondo)
Io mi glorio (binary)
Io non amo (rounded binary), 83
Io piangea (aria di piú parti)

O biondi tesori (binary with closing refrain)
Occhi ardenti (rondo)
Occhi belli, occhi miei (binary), 51, 70, 82, 130
Occhi belli, occhi vezzosi (binary with closing refrain)
Occhi quei vaghi (binary), 51, 75, 158
Occhi soavi (binary), 40, 76, 160
O cieli, pietà (binary), 39, 75, 90, 157
O dura piú d'un sasso (aria di piú parti)
O gradita libertà (aria di piú parti), 56, 93
O grotta, o speco (lament), 20
Ohime, madre (rounded binary), 34, 41, 63, 90, 107, 144
Olà, pensieri (rounded binary), 77, 127, 136, 138, 164
Ombre fuggite (aria di piú parti), 98
Orrida e solitaria (lament)

Partii dal gioire (binary), 122
Patienza, tocca a me (aria di piú parti)
Pender non prima (lament), 20
Pene, pianti e sospiri (binary with closing refrain)
Pensoso, afflitto (aria di piú parti)
Perche chieder (ternary), 41, 42, 77-78, 165
Perche ratto (binary), 61, 72, 141, 148, 166
Perche, speranze (aria di piú parti)
Piangea l'aurora (aria di piú parti)
Pietà, spietati lumi (binary), 91
Poiche mancò (binary with closing refrain)
Precorrea del sol (binary), 51, 58, 67, 70, 80
Presso un ruscel (aria di piú parti)
Pria ch'al sdegno (aria di piú parti)
Provai d'amor (binary)
Pur è ver (aria di piú parti), 24-25

Quand'io credo (ternary)
Quando Florinda (lament)
Quando meco tornerai (rondo), 155
Quando mi chiede (aria di piú parti)
Quando piú mia libertà (ternary), 83, 124
Quando spiega (binary with closing refrain), 41, 54-55, 80, 87
Quante volte (rounded binary), 51, 106, 109-10, 183
Quanto è credulo (rondo), 51, 99-100
Querelatevi di me (ternary), 60, 139
Queste dure catene (binary)
Questo piccolo rio (binary), 72, 87, 148, 177

The Simple Binary Cantatas

For Solo Voice

Acuto gelo
Addio, perfida
Al cenno d'una speranza
All'hor ch'il ben
Amor, così si fa
Amor s'io mi querelo
A tanti sospiri
Chi cercando va
Chi desia di salire
Chi mi credeva
Ch'io sospiri
Chiuda quest'occhi
  (Pasqualini's?)
Come è breve
Come tosto sparisce
Dissi un giorno
Diva, tu che in trono
Dopo lungo penare
D'una bella infedel
E può soffrirsi
Farfalletta che ten vai
  (Marazzoli's)
Già nel oblio
Hor ch'avvolte in fosco
Horche di marte
Hor ch'io vivo
Ho vinto, gridava
Il cor mi dice
Io che sin hor
Io ero pargoletta

For Ensemble

Ahi, quante volte
Al bel lume
Amanti, ardire
Amor con dolci vezzi
Apritevi, o begl'occhi
Bella bocca
Chi d'amor sin'a i capelli
Come sete importuni
Corilla danzando
Datemi pace
Deh, perche
Di capo ad Amarilli
Di desire in desire
Dite, o cieli
Due feroci guerrieri
Due labbra
Fan battaglia
Guardate dove va
Ha cent'occhi
In questo duro
Invan mi tendete
Io mi glorio
Lucciolette vaganti
  (Marazzoli's)
Mio cor, di che
Non cantar libertà
Non più strali
Occhi belli, occhi miei
Occhi quei vaghi
Occhi soavi

For Solo Voice	For Ensemble
La bella per cui	O cieli, pietà
Mai no'l dirò	Pietà, spietati lumi
Non m'affligete	Provai d'amor
Partii dal gioire	Questo dure catene
Perche ratto così	Si, o no
Precorrea del sol	Speranza, al tuo pallore
Questo piccolo rio	Tu giuri
Se dolente e flebil	Udite, amanti
Tenti e ardisca	Un amante se'n viene
Un pensier nobile	Un tiranno di foco
Voi sete troppo belle	Vorrei scoprirti

The Simple Binary Cantatas with Closing Refrain

For Solo Voice	For Ensemble
Amanti, piangete	Ahi, dunqu'è pur vero
A qual dardo	A i sospiri, al dolore
Armatevi d'orgoglio	Amor se devo
Deggio dunque in amore	Che non puote
De la vita	Che sospiri, martiri
Gelosia che a poco	Dolenti pensieri
Già finita è	Filli, non penso
Ho perduto la fortuna	Frena il pianto
Ingordo human	Lasso, benche
Luci belle	O biondi tesori
Lungi da me	Pene, pianti e sospiri
Mani alteri	Piansi già (Marazzoli's)
Misero cor	Poiche mancò
No, mio bene	Quasi baleno (Marazzoli's)
Occhi belli, occhi vezzosi	Sempre dunque
Quando spiega la notte	Viemmi, o sdegno
Ragion mi dice	
Se mai ti punge	
Se nell'arsura	
S'io son vinto	
Sognai, lasso	
Son divenuto	
Sparite dal core	

For Solo Voice

Spenti gl'affanni
Taci, ohime

For Ensemble

The Rondo Cantatas

For Solo Voice

A chi, lasso
Adorate mie catene
A me stesso
Amor giura
Che cosa mi dite
Che dici, mio core
Che farò, m'innamoro
Che sventura
Chi di voi
Chi non ha speranza
Chi non sa fingere
Ch'io speri
Chi trovasse
Come penare
Con amor e senza speme
Con amor si pugna
Con voi parlo
Così va
Deh, soccorri
Deh, soffri
Difendi, mio core
E chi non v'ameria
E si crede
Fanciulla son'io
Fate quel che volete
Guardatevi, olà
Hor guardate come va
Io lo vedo
La bella che mi contenta
La bella più bella
Luci mie
Mai finirò
Mi contento così

For Ensemble

Augellin di sete
Che pretendete
Chi può resister
Cor dolente
Libertà, ragion
Speranze, sentite
Tu sarai

For Solo Voice   **For Ensemble**

Ne notte ne dì
Nessun sene vanti
Non la volete
No, non ci pensa
Non sarà, non fu
Occhi ardenti
Quando meco tornerai
Quando è credulo
Sento al cor
Si v'ingannate
Sospiri, su, su
Speranze, che dite
Sulla veglia
Tra montagne

The Ternary Cantatas

For Solo Voice   **For Ensemble**

All'ombra d'una speranza   A te, mio core
Amor, e perche   Cor dolente
Begl'occhi, che dite   Disperate speranze
Difenditi, o core   Il contento che mi deste
E d'amore foll'inganno   Mortale, che pensi
Fanciulle tenete il guard'a voi   Mio core, impara dal mare
Non c'è che dire   Non mi lusingar più
Perche chieder com'io sto   Quand'io credo esser
Quando più mia libertà   Soffrirei con lieto core
Querelatevi di me   Su, su, begl'occhi
Un cor che non chiede aita   Tu parti, core, addio

The Rounded Binary Cantatas

For Solo Voice   **For Ensemble**

Armatevi di sdegno   Ho perso il mio core
Begl'occhi, pietà   Risolvetevi
Che vuoi più da me
Difenditi, amore
Disperati, che aspetti più

For Solo Voice	For Ensemble
Io non amo	
Mio core languisce	
M'uccidete, begl'occhi	
Non mi fate mentire	
Ohime, madre, aita	
Olà, pensieri, olà	
Quante volte l'ho detto	
Rendetevi, pensieri	
Respira, core	
Sei pur dolce, o libertà	
Su, su, mio core, la guerra	
Uscite di porto, pensieri	

The Arie Di Più Parti

For Solo Voice	For Ensemble
A la rota	Ardo, sospiro
Anime, voi che sete	Chi non sa
Atra notte	Compatite un cor
Benche roca pur impetra	E che pensi
Che tardi più	Horche fra l'ombre
Chi batte il mio core	Horch'in notturna pace
Da perfida	Horche notte guerriera
Dove più giro	Infelici pensier
E che cantar	Lo splendor
Ferma, Giove, ferma	Noi siam tre
Fillide mia	O gradita libertà
Fingi ch'io t'ho tradito	Piangea l'aurora
Giusto così	Pur è ver
Horche la notte	Rugge quasi leon
Horche l'oscuro	Sovra un lido
Hor si versate	Spiega un volo
Io piangea	
Lascia speranza	
Lasciate ch'io ritorni	
Lasciatemi qui solo	
Mentre sorge	
Mi danno la morte	
Mostro con l'ali	

For Solo Voice   **For Ensemble**

Non più viltà
O dura più d'un sasso
Ombre fuggite
Patienza tocca a me
Pensoso, afflitto
Perche, speranze
Presso un ruscel
Pria ch'al sdegno
Quando mi chiede
Ravvolse il volo
Satiatevi, o cieli
Se mi volete morto
Se non corre
S'era alquanto
Sopra conca
Sospiri miei
Sospiri, olà
Sparite dal volto
Su, consiglio
Torna indietro
Tornate, o miei (Marazzoli's)
Tutto cinto
V'è, v'è, che miro

The Laments

All'hor ch'il forte Alcide
Al soave spirar
Con occhi belli
Erminia sventurata
Hora ch'ad eclissar
In solitario
Nel dì ch'al Padre eterno
O grotta, o speco
Orrida e solitaria
Pender non prima
Quando Florinda
Rugge quasi leon
Sola fra i suoi
Sotto l'ombra d'un pino

Sparsa il crine
Tra romite contrade
Un ferito cavaliero

A Selection of the Cantatas

I. Se nell'arsura

Se nell'ar=sura ch'amor ti die=de, brami, gar=zon, di ristorarti alquanto, sce=ma dal cor la fede. Non amar tanto, no, non amar tanto, non amar tanto, no, non amar tanto! Dolce pa=stura di mobil co=re, fu' sempr'A=mo=

26 ... =re, ma che se n'empie è stol=to anco'l

33 dolce li=quor _____ nuoce s'è mol=

39 =to. Vuoi tu fuggir, vuoi tu fuggir d'una bellez=

43 adagio =za il fo=co? Ama poco, ama po=co,

47 ama po=co, ama po=co!

Texts for two strophic repetitions of the entire cantata:

II

Beltà che piace
agl'occhi tuoi
è lampo, è ver, ma non vi gire a canto
se fulmini non vuoi!
Non amar tanto!

Lucente face
d'ombroso core
fu sempre Amore.
Ma se rischiara accende
fiamma ch'appaga i lumi il tatto offende.
Vuoi tu fuggir d'una bellezza il foco?
Ama poco, ama poco!

III

Se in mesta vita
languendo stai,
mira un bel viso e sanerai del pianto,
ma non stiarne i rai!
Non amar tanto!

Tranquilla aita
d'afflitto core
fu sempre Amore.
Ma nell'infermo seno
smisurato rimedio anco e veleno.
Ama poco, ama poco!

II. Quando spiega la notte

*F sharp and no tie in Rés. Vm⁷ 102;
tie and no sharp in Harl. 1265.

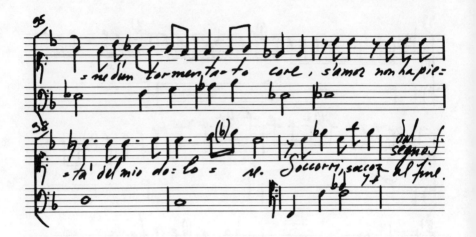

s ne d'un tormenta=to core, s'amor non ha pie=

=tà del mio do:lo=   re. Soccormi, soccor al fine.

III. Difenditi, amore

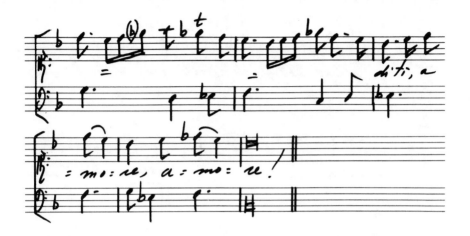

The texts of the second and third stanzas of the second unit are given in chapter 2, pp. 35–36.

IV. Disperati, che aspetti

ode, cordoglio non vede di chi langue in ser ri=

=tù. Preghiera non ode, cordoglio non vede di chi

langue in ser = = ristù. Dispe=rati,

di=spe=ra=ti, ch'aspetti più, dispe=ra=ti, che

chi'a= spetti più!

Fine

Text for the strophic repetition of the entire cantata:

Acquetati, non v'è pietà!
Di mendicata fede
non sa mai donar mercede
chi si fallace
finse la pace
per tradir l'altrui bontà.
Acquetati, non v'e pietà!

Tutto ridente
all'hor che mente
che cosa dal unge[1]
dolor non la punge
memoria non l'ange
di chi move a sua beltà.
Acquetati, non v'e pietà!

1. I am not sure of the last three syllables of this verse; the script is difficult to read.

V. Respira, core

Text for the strophic repetition of the second unit:

Minaccia invano
questa cometa,
al fine e meta
divina mano.
Oh Dio, o Dio!
Lasso cor mio,
scaccia il dolore.
Respira, core!   da capo[1]

1. The two sources that give this text have the rubric "da capo" at the close of the
final verse.

VI. Uscite di porto

to, u- sci- te di- por = = to. = to, u- sci- te di por - to. = to, u-scite di por to.

Second and third stanzas for the strophic repetition of the second unit:

II

Timor non v'assaglia
che barbare prove.
Schierate in battaglia
minaccino il core.
Chi servo è d'amore
guerriero costante,
non cangia sembiante
o timido, o smorto.
Uscite di porto!

III

Lasciate del petto
in guardia la fede.
E dolce diletto
sia vostra mercede.
Desir che non cede
per tema d'affanni,
gioisce ne danni
dall'anima scorto.
Uscite di porto!

VII. Difenditi, o core

Difenditi o core, difen=diti o core, per
lampo fu=gace si perde la pace, si ge=me, si
muo=re, per lampo fugace si perde la pace, si
ge=me, si muore. Difenditi o core, difen=diti o
core, difen= :di=ti o co=re.

fine

= ma che mo = = re. Dio

Sen diti o core ut supra
al fine

VIII. Che cosa mi dite

Che cosa mi dite? Che si cangi = =no in con=tenti i tormen-ti che sof=frite? Che cosa mi dite? Che co= = -sa, che co= sa mi di = te? Già sette volte il sol per gl'emisferi dallo: case è trascorso in O=ri=ente. ne

Second stanza for the second unit:

La catena d'amor sempre è catena,
ne si v'afferma in gioie un aspro affanno.
Cupido tiranno
s'è fatto sirena.
V'alletterà coi guardi,
vi mostrerà d'un crin gli cor bugiardi.
Dirà che l'amante
vuol esser costante,
che godrete se languite.

Che cosa mi dite
....Continue with the refrain as after
   the first stanza.

IX. Hor guardate

Second stanza for the second unit:

Troppo chiaro è del sole
l'infelice tormento.
Ecco Dafne non vuole
fuggitiva ascoltar prieghi o lamento.
E pur possible è
che non gi dia merce,
anzi in un tronco ella cangiar si fa.
Hor guardate come va!
E pur possibile è
che non gli dia merce,
anzi in un tronco ella cangiar si fa!

Hor guardate come va!
....Continue with the refrain as after the
    first stanza.

X. Precorrea del sol

macchie=ro. Pien il lido è di spavento, fischia

l'on : = : = da

e mugghia il vento, e mugghia il ven = :

=to.

3ª

Al soffiar ———— d'Euro che freme

s'empie il ciel d'horro=re e lutto. Vo= la il

fluto e del mar ____ l'a=rena ge= me,

vo= =la il fluto e del mar ____ l'a

=re=na ge = me. Van' tra scogli ilegni infranti.

e dar' for -

= =za all'onde i pian=

56   76   57

= ra do = na. Quest'il mare è di Capido,

deh, non sia, deh, non sia chi la = = sci'l

li = do, deh, non sia chi la = =

= sci il li = do.

XI. Non mi fate mentire

Text for the strophic repetition of the entire cantata:

Non celate piú il vero!
Dite pur se mi amate,
o mio tesoro,
se non lo dite, io moro;
se lo celate, io pero.
Non celate piú il vero!

Troppo grave e il dolore
che va struggendo il core
di chi brama sentir vostro pensiero.
Non celate piú il vero!

XII. Amor, e perche

ma-le.

Il pianto non vale, servir non mi giova, ser-

vir non mi gio-va che mai non si trova mercede per me.

=mo, e perche? da capo (al fine)

XIII. Risolvetevi, o martiri

XIV. Speranze, sentite

Prima solo

76

voi che fuste solo la cagion ch'io venni a=man=te, senza voi che fuste solo la cagion ch'io venni a=man=te, ch'io ven= =ni a=man=te.

Deh, fermate almen le piante nel mio cor, benche tra= =di=to son'a un cor d'amor feri=to, le lu= singhe anco gra di= te, son a un cor d'amor fe= ri to,

(**)

le lu= singhe an=co gra di= te, lo lusin=

Speranze   da capo

=ghe anco gra=di = te.

XV. E può soffrirsi

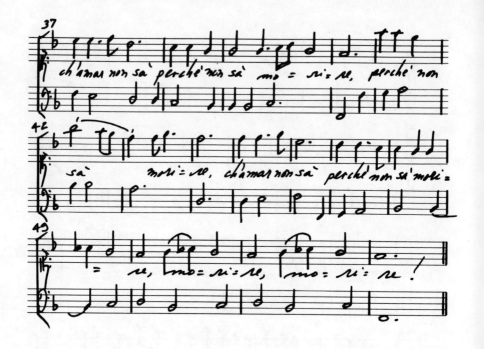

XVI. Taci, ohime

Text for the strophic repetition of the entire cantata:

Lasso, ohime, non v'è pietà!
La crudel ond'io mi moro,
quando amante piú l'adoro,
con fierezza
mi disprezza
e cruda sta.
Lasso, ohime, non v'e pietà!

Hor va, languisci,
incenerisci,
sventurato, e che piú vuoi?
Far non puoi
che dia merce!
Le dolcezze d'amor non son per me!

XVII. Mi contento, the refrain

XVIII. M'uccidete, the first unit

XIX. Il contento, the second unit

XX. Lungi da me

Lun=gi da me, mio be = ne. i=do=lo di quest' al = = = ma con te=naci cate=ne nel ser=vaggio d'a = :mor por = = = to la pal=ma, por= : to la pal=ma, con te=naci ca=

25
=tene nel ser=raggio d'a=mor por

= to la pal=ma. Li=bertà per

mo non cu=ro, anzi li=bero

mo = =ni=

=re=i, sol pe=nan=do m'as=si=

=cu=ro di be=a=re i gior=ni mi=ei, sol pe=

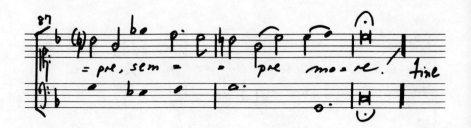

Texts for two strophic repetitions of the entire cantata:

II

Son d'un anima amante
degno cibo i sospiri.
Una lagrima errante
è soverchio contento a miei martiri.

Se talhor pensier geloso
del mio ben m'affligge il core,
con affetto generoso
vo beando il mio dolore.

Fugga il regno d'amor chi non ha core,
e sol vive in amor chi sempre more!

III

Chi non ama penando
non conosce il gioire.
Tra le fiamme vagando
provo più fortunato il mio morire.

Benche sia lunge il mio foco
ho vicino il mio tormento;
il gioire a poco a poco
è un durabile contento.

Fugga il regno d'amor chi non ha core,
e sol vive in amor chi sempre more!

XXI. Pietà, spietati lumi

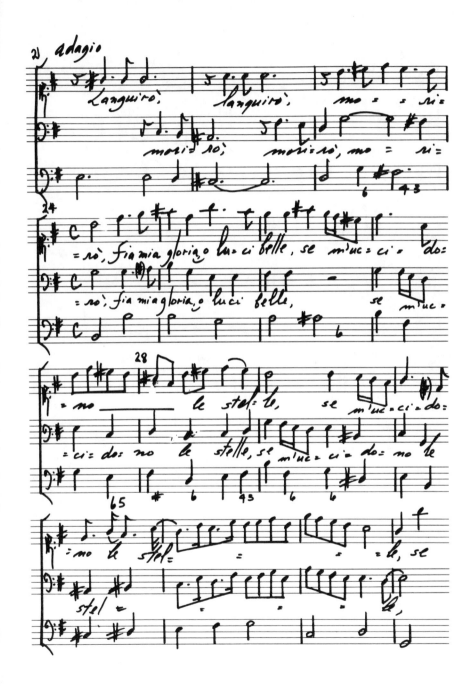

XXII. Torna indietro, the first arietta

XXIII. Quando più, mia libertà, the second unit

E ragion forte guerriera, m'abbandona e rinta ce=de. Una speme lusinghiera tnion=far di lei si ve=de, il desir che le fà guer=

XXIV. Non mi lusingar

XXV. Non m'affligete

XXVI. Quanto è credulo, the refrain

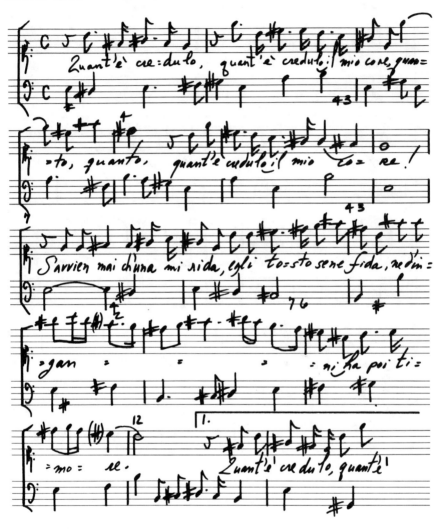

. to,   Quant'è   cre =

= duto il mio co=re, il

43

— gio   co= re!

XXVII. Speranze, che dite

(Fine)

faccia fe=ni=tà. Speranze, che dite, an=

cosa credete, ancora, ancora cre=de=

=te? Andate   da capo
              as before

Bibliography

This bibliography covers the thematic catalogue as well as the main text.

Abbiati, Franco. *Storia della Musica*, vol. II. Milano: Garzanti, 1946.

Abert, Anna Amalie. "Cesti." *MGG* II (1952), cols. 989-996.

Alaleona, D. "Le Laudi spirituali italiane nei secoli XVe, XVIe, XVIIe; il loro rapporto coi canti profani." *RMI* XVI (1909): I.

Aldrich, Putnam. *Rhythm in Seventeenth-Century Italian Monody*. New York: W. W. Norton, 1966.

Andrews, Hilda. *Catalogue of the King's Music Library*. Vol. II: *The Miscellaneous Manuscripts*. London, 1929.

Arkwright, Godfrey Edward P. *Catalogue of Music in the Library of Christ Church, Oxford*. Part I: *Works of Ascertained Authorship*. Oxford, 1915. Part II: *Ms. Works of Unknown Authorship, (i) Vocal*. Oxford, 1923.

Associazione dei Musicologi Italiani. *Catalogo delle Opere Esistenti nelle Biblioteche e negli Archivi Publici e Privati d'Italia*. Volumes IV, VI, VIII and X. Parma, respectively, 1929, 1914, 1913, and 1934.

Baronci, G. *Inventario dei codici Barberini musicali*. MS, 1931-32. I Rvat, Sala Cons. MS 381.

Beccherini, Bianca. *Catalogo dei Manoscritti Musicali della Biblioteca Nazionale di Firenze*. Kassel, 1959.

Buff, Iva Moore. "The Chamber Duets and Trios of Carissimi." Unpublished Ph.D. dissertation, University of Rochester, 1973.

Burney, Charles. *A General History of Music from the Earliest Ages to the Present Period*. 4 vols. London, 1776-1789. Edition edited by Frank Mercer. 2 vols. New York, 1957.

Burrows, David Lamont. "The Cantatas of Antonio Cesti." Unpublished Ph.D. dissertation, Brandeis University, 1961.

_____, ed. *The Italian Cantata, I. Antonio Cesti*. Wellesley, 1963.

_____. *Antonio Cesti. Wellesley Edition Cantata Index Series*. Fascicle 1. Wellesley College, 1964.

_____. "Antonio Cesti on Music," *The Musical Quarterly* LI (1965): 518 ff.

Caluori, Eleanor. "Luigi Rossi." *The New Grove Dictionary of Music and Musicians* XVI: 217-221. London, 1980.

Cametti, Alberto. "Alcuni documenti inediti su la vita di Luigi Rossi compositore di musica (1597-1653)." *SIMG* XIV (1912-13): 1-26.

_____. *Musicisti Celebri del Seicento in Roma: Marc' Antonio Pasqualini*. Milan, 1921. (Extract from *Musica d'Oggi* N. 3-4, 1921.)

_____. "Orazio Michi Dell'Arpa." *RMI* XXI (1914): 203-277.

Capponi, Piero. "Marco Marazzoli e l'Oratorio *Cristo e i Farisei*." *La Scuola Romana*, pp. 101-106. Siena, 1953.

Carissimi, Giacomo. *Ars Cantandi. See* Douglas, James.

Catalogo delle Arie, Duetti, Madrigali e Cantate, con stromenti diversi e con cembalo solo, che si trovano in manoscritto nella Officina Musica di Giovanni Gottlob Immanuel Breitkopf. Parte VI. Leipzig, 1765.

Celani, Enrico. "Canzoni musicale del secolo XVII." *RMI* II (1905): 109–150.

Chaikin, Kathleen. "The Solo Cantatas of Alessandro Stradella." Unpublished Ph.D. dissertation, Stanford University, 1975.

Cicognini, Andrea. *Orontea, Regina d'Egitto*. Venetia, n.d.; Firenze, 1661; Torino, 1662; Venetia, 1666.

Cognasso, Francesco. *Storia di Torino*. Torino, 1934.

Crain, Gordon. "The Vocal Music of Bernardo Pasquini." Unpublished Ph.D. dissertation, Yale University, 1964.

Croce, Benedetto. *Storia dell'Età Barocca in Italia*. Bari, 1957.

Douglas, James; trans. "The Art of Singing." A translation in English of *Ars Cantandi* from an edition of 1693 of a German translation of the original in Italian by Giovanni Giacomo Carissimi. A photostat of the 1693 edition accompanies the translation. Unpublished thesis, Master of Sacred Music, Union Theological Seminary, 1949.

Ecorcheville, Jules. *Catalogue du Fonds de Musique Ancienne de la Bibliothèque Nationale*. 8 vols. Paris, 1910-1914.

Eisley, Irving. "The Secular Cantatas of Mario Savioni (1608–1685)." Unpublished Ph.D. dissertation, University of California, Los Angeles, 1964.

_____. *Mario Savioni. The Wellesley Edition Cantata Index Series*. Fascicle 2. Wellesley College, 1964.

Eitner, Robert. *Biographisch-Bibliographisches Quellen-Lexikon der Musiker und Musikgelehrten der christlichen Zeitrechnung bis zur Mitte des neunzehnten Jahrhunderts*. 10 vols. Leipzig, 1900–1904.

Fétis, François Joseph. *Biographie Universelle des Musiciens et Bibliographie Générale de la Musique*. 8 vols. 2d ed., Paris, 1860–1865.

Fortune, Nigel. "Italian Secular Monody from 1600 to 1635." *MQ* (April, 1958), pp. 145-166.

Frescobaldi, Girolamo. *Arie Musicali*. Florence, 1630.

Fuller-Maitland, John A., and Arthur H. Mann. *Catalogue of the Music in the Fitzwilliam Museum, Cambridge*. London, 1893.

Gaspari, Gaetano. *Catalogo della Biblioteca del Liceo Musicale di Bologna*. 5 vols. Bologna, 1890–1943.

Ghislanzoni, Alberto. *Luigi Rossi. Biografia e Analisi delle Composizioni*. Milan, 1954.

Greenberg, Noah; ed. *An Elizabethan Song Book*. Doubleday Anchor: New York, 1955.

Grout, Donald Jay. *A Short History of Opera*. One-volume edition. New York, 1947.

Hanley, Edwin. "Alessandro Scarlatti's *Cantate da Camera*; A Bibliographical Study." Yale University, 1963.

Holmes, William. "Rossi, Luigi." *MGG* XI (1963), cols. 938–942.

Hudson, Barton. "Notes on Gregorio Strozzi and his *Capricci*." *JAMS* XX, No. 2 (1967), pp. 209-221.

Hudson, Richard. "The Passacaglia and Ciaccona in Italian Keyboard Music of the 17th Century." *The Diapason* (Nov., 1969): 22-24; (Dec., 1969): 6-7.

Hughes-Hughes, Augustus. *Catalogue of Manuscript Music in the British Museum*. 3 vols. London, 1906, 1908, 1909.

Israel, Karl. *Uebersichtlicher Katalog der Musikalien der staendischen Landesbibliotehk zu Kassel*. Kassel, 1881.

Jander, Owen. "The Works of Alessandro Stradella Related to the Cantata and the Opera." Unpublished Ph.D. dissertation, Harvard University, 1962.

_____. *Alessandro Stradella. Wellesley Edition Cantata Index Series*. Fascicles 4a and 4b. Wellesley College, 1969.

Jonckbloet, W.J.A., and J.P.N. Land; eds. *Musique et Musiciens au XVIIe Siècle*. Leyden, 1882.

Kade, Otto. *Die Musikalien-Sammlung des Grossherzoglich Mecklenberg. Schweriner Fuerstenhauses.* 2 vols. Schwerin, 1893.

Kast, Paul. "Domenico Mazzocchi." *MGG* VIII (1960), cols. 1862–1866.

──────. "Marco Marazzoli." *MGG* VIII (1960), cols. 1611–1613.

Knolles, Richard. *The Turkish History from the Original of that Nation to the Growth of the Ottoman Empire with the Lives and Conquests of their Princes and Emperors.* 3 vols. Awnsham Churchill: London, 1687.

Limentani, Uberto; ed. *Poesie e Lettere Inedite di Salvator Rosa.* Firenze, Olschki, 1950.

Lotti, Giovanni. *Poesi Latine, e Toscane, date in luce da Ambrogio Lancellotti suo nipote.* Roma: Gio. Giacomo Komarek bohemo, 1688.

Mariani, Lucilla. "Le 18 canzonette di un codice musicale del '600." *Accademie e Bibliotheche d'Italia* VIII (1934): 145–169.

Marino, Cavalier (Gianbattista). *La Lira, Rime.* 3 vols. in 1. Ventia: Gio Battista Ciotti, 1629.

Monteverdi, Claudio. *12 Composizioni Vocali Profane e Sacre* (Inedite), ed. Wolfgang Osthoff. Milano, Ricordi, 1958.

Morgan, Lady Sydney. *The Life and Times of Salvator Rosa.* 2 vols., London, 1824.

Morris, Robert B. "A Study of the Italian Solo Cantata Before 1750." Unpublished dissertation, Doctor of Music Education, Indiana University, 1955.

Murata, Margaret. "Further Remarks on Pasqualini and the Music of MAP." *Analecta Musicologica* XIX (1976): 125–145.

──────. "The Recitative Soliloquy." *JAMS* XXXII (1979): 43–73.

Noack, Elizabeth. "Dialog." *MGG* III (1954), cols. 391–403.

Ott, Alfons. "Musikbibliotheken und Sammlungen." *MGG* IX (1961), cols. 1034–1078.

Palisca, Claude, "Bonini." *MGG* III (1952), cols. 107–109.

──────. "Vincenzo Galilei and Some Links Between 'Pseudo-Monody' and Monody." *MQ* (July, 1960), pp. 344 ff.

Parry, Charles. *The Oxford History of Music.* Vol. III. *The Music of the Seventeenth Century.* 2d ed. London, 1938.

Piantanida, Sandro, Lamberto Diotallevi and Giancarlo Livraghi; eds. *Autori Italiani del '600.* 4 vols. Milano, 1948–1952.

Pirrotta, Nino. "Tre Capitoli su Cesti. II. *L'Orontea.*" *La Scuola Romana.* Siena, 1953.

Prunières, Henry. "Catalogue des manuscrits italiens de cantatas des XVIIe et XVIIIe siècles de la bibliothèque de M. Henry Prunières à Paris." Typewritten booklet, n.d., at the New York Public Library.

──────. "Notes bibliographiques sur les cantates de Luigi Rossi au Conservatoire de Naples." *ZIMG* XVI 4 (1913): 109–111.

──────. *L'Opéra Italien en France avant Lulli.* Paris: Champion, 1913.

──────. "La cantata italienne à voix seule au dix-septième siècle." *Encyclopédie de la Musique et Dictionnaire du Conservatoire.* Part II. Vol. V. Paris, 1913–1939, pp. 3390–3410.

──────. "Les représentations du Palazzo d'Atlante à Rome (1642), d'après des documents inédits." *SIMG* XIV (1912–1913): 218–226.

──────. "Notes sur la vie de Luigi Rossi (1598–1653)." *SIMG* XII (1910-1911): 12-16.

Raschl, Erich. "Die weltlichen Vokalwerke des Giovanni Felice Sances, ca. 1600–1679." Unpublished Ph.D. dissertation, University of Graz, 1968.

Répertoire International des Sources Musicales. Vol. I. *Recueils Imprimés, XVIe-XVIIe Siècles.* I. Liste Chronologique. G. Henle: Muenchen-Duisburg, 1960.

Ricci, Vittorio; ed. *Antiche Gemme Italiane.* Milano: Ricordi, 1949.

Riemann, Hugo. *Handbuch der Musikgeschichte.* Zweiter Band, Zweiter Teil. Leipzig: Breitkopf und Haertel, 1922.

Rolland, Roman. *Musiciens d'autrefois.* pp. 55-105. Paris, 1908.

Rosand, Ellen. "Barbara Stozzi, *virtuosissima cantatrice,*" *JAMS* (1978): 241-281.

Rose, Gloria. "The Cantatas of Carissimi." Unpublished Ph.D. dissertation, Yale University, 1959.

————. "The Cantatas of Giacomo Carissimi," MQ XLVIII (1962): 207 ff. 207 ff.

————. *Giacomo Carissimi. Wellesley Edition Cantata Index Series.* Fascicle 5. Wellesley College, 1966.

————. "Pasqualini as Copyist." *Analecta Musicologica* XIV (1974): 170-175.

————. "The Italian Cantata of the Baroque Period." *Schrade Festschrift.* Berne: Francke, 1973: 655-677.

Rossi, Luigi. *Il Palazzo Incantato.* Reproduction of MS copy in I Rvat, Chigi Q V 51 with introduction by Howard Mayer Brown. New York: Garland Publishers, 1977.

Rubsamen, Walter H. *"Music Research in Italian Libraries."* Music Library Association Notes VI (1949) : 220-223, 543-569; VIII (1950): 70-99.

Sartori, Claudio. *"The Wellesley Edition Cantata Index Series."* Book review. *Notes* (June, 1967): 734-737.

Schering, Arnold. *Geschichte der Musik in Beispielen.* Leipzig, 1913.

Schlitzer, Franco. "Fortuna dell'*Orontea.*" *La Scuola Romana.* Siena, 1953, pp. 81-92.

Schmidl, Carlo. *Dizionario Universale dei Musicisti.* 3 vols. Milano, 1929.

Schmitz, Eugen. *Geschichte der weltlichen Solokantate.* 2d ed., Leipzig, 1955.

Silbiger, Alexander. "The Roman Frescobaldi Tradition." *JAMS* XXXIII (1980): 42-87.

————. *Italian Manuscript Sources of 17th-Century Keyboard Music.* Ann Arbor: UMI Research Press, 1979.

Smith, Norman E. "The Cantatas of Luigi Rossi; the Christ Church Manuscripts." Unpublished seminar paper, Yale University, 1955.

Smither, Howard E. "The Latin Dramatic Dialogue and the Nascent Oratorio." *JAMS* XX (Fall, 1967): 403-443.

Solerti, Angelo. *Le Origini del Melodramma; Testimonianze dei Contemporanei.* Torino, 1903.

Sonneck, Oscar. *Library of Congress. Catalogue of Opera Librettos Printed Before 1800.* Vol. I. *Title Catalogue.* Washington, 1914.

Squire, W. Barclay. *Catalogue of Printed Music Published Between 1478 and 1800 Now in the British Museum.* 2 vols. London, 1912.

Steffani, Agostino. *Ausgewaehlte Werke, Erster Teil.* Edited by Alfred Einstein and Adolf Sandberger, in *Denkmaeler der Tonkunst in Bayern* VI, 2. Leipzig, 1905.

Tagliavini, Luigi Ferdinando. "Rosa, Salvatore." *MGG* XI (1963), cols. 902-903.

Timms, Colin. "The chamber duets of Agostino Steffani 1654-1728." Unpublished Ph.D. dissertation, University of London, 1976.

Torchi, Luigi. "Canzoni ed Arie italiane ad una voce nel secolo XVII." *RMI* I (1894): 581-656.

————, ed. *Eleganti canzoni ed arie italiane del secolo XVIII.* Milan, 1893.

Torrefranca, Fausto. "Mazarin." *MGG* VIII (1960), cols. 1853-1854.

Villari, Luigi. "Savoy, House of." *Encyclopaedia Brittanica*, 1958 edition, Vol. XX: 24-27.

Villari, Pasquale. "Medici." *Encyclopaedia Brittanica*, 1958 edition, Vol. XV: 189-194.

Vogel, Emil and Alfred Einstein. *Biblioteca della Musica Vocale Italiana di Genere Profano, Stampata dal 1500 al 1700.* 2 vols. Hildesheim, Georg Olms, 1962.

Walker, Frank. "Salvator Rosa and Music. I. Burney and Rosa's supposed compositions: II. Music and Musicians in Rosa's letters." *Monthly Musical Record* LXXIX (October, 1949): 199-205, and LXXX (January and February, 1950): 13-16 and 32-36.

Walker, Thomas. "Ciaccona and Passacaglia: Remarks on Their Origin and Early History." *JAMS* XXI (Fall, 1968): 300–320.

Welter, Friedrich. *Katalog der Musikalien der Ratsbuecherei Lueneburg.* Lippstadt, 1950.

Witzenmann, Wolfgang. "Autographe Marco Marazzolis in der Biblioteca Vaticana." *Analecta Musicologica* VII (1968): 36–86 and IX (1970): 203–294.

Wotquenne, Alfred. *Catalogue de la Bibliothèque du Conservatoire de Musique de Bruxelles.* 5 vols. Brussels, 1894–1914.

—————. *Etude Bibliographique sur le compositeur napolitain Luigi Rossi (-1653).* Brussels, 1909.

Index